Cyber Security Blueprint

Your Definitive Guide to Launching a
Successful Career

AFRIN SHAIK

Blueprint: Your Definitive Guide to Launching a Successful Career"

Afrin Shaik has no responsibility for the persistence or accuracy of the URLs for the external or third-party internet websites referred to in this publication and does not guarantee that any content on such websites is, or will remain, accurate or appropriate.

First edition

For more information, afrin.shaik18@gmail.com

ISBN PIN : 9798873541478

Contents

Preface

Welcome to the exploration of "Cybersecurity Blueprint: "Your Definitive Guide to Launching a Successful Career." In the vast expanse of the digital realm, the significance of cybersecurity has become more pronounced than ever. This book is not just a compilation of technical details; it is a carefully curated guide aimed at illuminating your path through the intricate world of cybersecurity and empowering you to embark on a fulfilling and impactful career.

As we navigate the pages of this guide, we delve into the dynamic landscape of cybersecurity, where challenges and opportunities evolve in tandem with technological advancements. Beyond the binary code, we recognize the holistic nature of this profession, considering the interplay between technology, human behaviour, and organizational dynamics. This book strives to equip you with not only technical proficiency but also the soft skills, ethical considerations, and strategic thinking essential for success in the cybersecurity domain.

Drawing from collective experiences gained through years of navigating the cybersecurity terrain, this guide provides strategic insights into threat landscapes, risk management, compliance frameworks, and emerging technologies. Each chapter serves as a waypoint, offering valuable perspectives to help you chart your course in this dynamic field.

This book is more than a theoretical guide—it's a practical toolkit designed to empower you on your journey. Through real-world examples, actionable advice, and hands-on exercises, we aim to equip you with the skills and knowledge needed to tackle the challenges of the cybersecurity profession. Whether you're honing technical expertise, refining communication skills, or developing a strategic mindset, this toolkit serves as your companion in success.

As you turn the pages of "Cybersecurity Blueprint," consider this not just a guide but a call to action. The challenges within the cybersecurity domain are dynamic and ever-evolving, but so are the opportunities for those prepared to seize them. Your journey into cybersecurity is not just about launching a career; it's about embracing a calling, becoming a guardian of the digital realm.

Your odyssey starts here. Are you ready to navigate the intricate pathways of cybersecurity and launch a career that transcends the digital frontier? Let this blueprint be your guide as you embark on this exciting and transformative journey.

Afrin Shaik

1st Jan 2024

Website: afrinshaik.dorik.io

Acknowledgments

In the journey of crafting "Cybersecurity Blueprint: Your Definitive Guide to Launching a Successful Career," numerous individuals and resources have contributed immeasurably to the realization of this project. This endeavour is a collective effort, and I extend my deepest gratitude to those whose support and expertise have made this book possible.

To my mentors and colleagues in the cybersecurity field, thank you for sharing your wealth of knowledge and experiences. Your insights have enriched the content of this guide and provided invaluable perspectives on the challenges and triumphs within the cybersecurity landscape.

A heartfelt appreciation goes to the cybersecurity community, whose collaborative spirit and commitment to knowledge-sharing form the bedrock of our profession. The vibrant discussions, forums, and shared resources have been instrumental in shaping the comprehensive nature of this guide.

I express my sincere thanks to the educators and institutions dedicated to nurturing the next generation of cybersecurity professionals. Your commitment to fostering learning environments and cultivating a passion for cybersecurity has laid the foundation for the individuals who will carry the torch forward.

Special gratitude is extended to the reviewers and contributors who dedicated their time and expertise to ensure the accuracy and relevance of the information presented in this guide. Your meticulous attention to detail and constructive feedback have undoubtedly enhanced the quality of the content.

To my family and friends, thank you for your unwavering support and understanding during the process of bringing this guide to fruition. Your encouragement has been a source of inspiration, and I am grateful for the encouragement that propelled me through the challenges of this endeavour.

Lastly, to the readers embarking on their cybersecurity journey through the pages of this guide, I extend my sincerest wishes for success. May the insights shared within these pages empower you to navigate the dynamic landscape of cybersecurity and launch a rewarding and impactful career.

This book is the result of a collaborative effort, and I am deeply appreciative of the diverse contributions that have shaped its content. Thank you to everyone who has been a part of this journey.

Introduction

Unveiling the Digital Guardianship Journey

In the symphony of ones and zeros that orchestrates our interconnected world, the silent sentinels of cybersecurity stand guard, warding off digital adversaries and ensuring the integrity of our digital existence. "Cybersecurity Blueprint: A Strategic Guide to Launching Your Career" is more than a guidebook; it's a gateway to a dynamic realm where code becomes a language of protection and resilience.

The Digital Frontier Awaits

As we venture into the heart of this blueprint, envision a digital frontier ripe with challenges and teeming with possibilities. The digital landscape is not just a canvas of vulnerabilities; it's an evolving canvas that invites you to become an architect of security, a guardian of the digital realm. This guide is your invitation to embark on a transformative journey into the world of cybersecurity.

Beyond Code: The Holistic Cybersecurity Professional

While codes and algorithms are the bricks and mortar of cybersecurity, this blueprint advocates for a holistic approach that transcends the binary. Beyond the lines of code lies an intricate tapestry of human behaviour, ethics, and strategic thinking. It beckons you to not only master the language of machines but also to understand the nuances of human actions and organizational dynamics.

Strategic Insights, Career Acceleration

Embedded within these pages are not just insights but strategic keys to unlock the doors to a successful cybersecurity career. Journey through the threat landscapes, unravel the mysteries of risk management, and explore emerging technologies that shape the cybersecurity horizon. This is your arsenal, your toolkit for career acceleration in a field where adaptability is as vital as technical prowess.

Your Cybersecurity Odyssey: A Call to Action

This isn't just a guide; it's a call to action. It beckons you to be the architect of your cybersecurity odyssey. The challenges you encounter are not hurdles but opportunities to grow, learn, and carve your niche in this dynamic landscape. The "Cybersecurity Blueprint" is your compass, guiding you through uncharted territories and empowering you to shape the future of digital security.

The Journey Commences

The odyssey into cybersecurity begins now. Are you ready to not just launch a career but to become a custodian of the digital age? "Cybersecurity Blueprint" is not just a book; it's your guidebook, your companion in this exhilarating journey. Let's embark on this transformative odyssey together, where every line of code written is a step towards fortifying the digital frontiers of tomorrow.

Who should read this book?

"Cybersecurity Blueprint: Your Definitive Guide to Launching a Successful Career" is tailored for a diverse audience, encompassing students, freshers, and professionals, all sharing a common passion for cybersecurity and a desire to excel in the digital guardianship realm. This book is specifically beneficial for:

Students and Recent Graduates: Whether you're currently pursuing a degree in cybersecurity or have just graduated, this guide serves as an essential companion. It provides a solid foundation for understanding the nuances of cybersecurity and offers practical insights to kickstart your journey toward a successful career.

Aspiring Cybersecurity Professionals: Individuals who are intrigued by the world of cybersecurity and are eager to carve out a path in this dynamic field will find this guide indispensable. It caters to those who are just beginning to explore the possibilities within cybersecurity, offering guidance on building the necessary skills and knowledge.

Tech Enthusiasts and Innovators: If you have a passion for technology and innovation and are curious about how these elements intersect with strategic thinking in cybersecurity, this book provides insights into the transformative power of technology within the context of safeguarding digital landscapes.

Seasoned Professionals Seeking Advancement: Experienced cybersecurity professionals looking to refine their strategic mindset, expand their skill set, or explore new dimensions within the field will discover valuable perspectives and practical advice to propel their careers to new heights.

Educators and Mentors: Teachers, professors, and mentors involved in educating and guiding the next generation of cybersecurity professionals will find this book to be a valuable resource. It provides insights and tools to enhance educational curricula and mentorship programs.

Leaders and Decision-Makers: Executives, managers, and decision-makers responsible for cybersecurity within organizations can gain a deeper understanding of the cybersecurity ecosystem. The guide offers strategic insights to inform decision-making, ensuring organizations are well-prepared to face digital threats.

Curious Minds Ready for a Challenge: Individuals with a curious mindset, a hunger for continuous learning, and a readiness to embrace challenges will find this book engaging. It presents cybersecurity as a thrilling domain where each chapter unfolds new possibilities, and every challenge becomes an opportunity for growth.

In essence, "Cybersecurity Blueprint" welcomes students, freshers, and professionals alike, offering a comprehensive guide to navigate and excel in the ever-evolving landscape of cybersecurity. Whether you're just beginning your journey or seeking to advance your career, this guide provides valuable insights and practical guidance for success in the cybersecurity domain.

About the Author

The author of "Cybersecurity Blueprint: Your Definitive Guide to Launching a Successful Career" is **Afrin Shaik**—a seasoned professional with over a decade of experience in keeping digital information safe. This means she has been actively involved in dealing with cyber threats, mastering ethical hacking, and contributing to strategies that safeguard organizations from online attacks.

But this book isn't just a technical manual. The author understands that excelling in cybersecurity involves more than just technical know-how. It's about having strong communication skills, ethical thinking, and the ability to plan smart strategies. You'll find these key aspects emphasized throughout "Cybersecurity Blueprint."

Beyond her work, the author enjoys sharing her knowledge with others in the cybersecurity community. This book is an extension of her desire to help people like you learn and thrive in the dynamic world of cybersecurity.

So, as you delve into "Cybersecurity Blueprint," think of the author as a friendly guide—a mentor who's been through the ropes in cybersecurity. She is here to share her wealth of knowledge, and this book is crafted to make your journey into the exciting realm of cybersecurity both informative and enjoyable. You can connect with **Afrin Shaik** via the following channels:

Website: afrinshaik.dorik.io

LinkedIn: https://www.linkedin.com/in/afrin-shaik-0bb6748b

Email: afrin.shaik18@gmail.com

How is this book structured?

Chapter 1: Introduction to the Cyber World

Embark on your cybersecurity journey with a comprehensive introduction to the cyber world. This chapter sets the stage, providing a foundational understanding of the digital landscape. Explore the significance of cybersecurity in today's interconnected society and grasp the fundamental concepts that will be the building blocks of your knowledge in the chapters to come. Get ready to unravel the mysteries and complexities of the cyber world.

Chapter 2: Assessing you Skills and Interests

Embark on a journey of self-discovery as we delve into assessing your skills and interests. This chapter guides you through a comprehensive process of evaluating your technical strengths and personal inclinations, laying the groundwork for a tailored approach to your cybersecurity career.

Chapter 3: Crafting Your Learning Path

In this chapter, we navigate the intricacies of designing a personalized learning path tailored to your cybersecurity aspirations. From foundational principles to advanced techniques, we'll explore the resources, courses, and certifications essential for acquiring the knowledge and skills needed in your evolving cybersecurity career. Craft a roadmap that aligns with your goals, ensuring a purposeful and effective learning journey.

Chapter 4: Building a Solid Foundation

Establish a rock-solid foundation for your cybersecurity endeavours. This chapter focuses on the fundamental principles and core concepts that underpin the field. From understanding encryption to grasping networking essentials, we'll lay the groundwork necessary for you to navigate the complexities of cybersecurity with confidence and proficiency. Solidify your knowledge base and set the stage for advanced exploration in subsequent chapters.

Chapter 5: Mastering Cybersecurity Tools

Dive into the arsenal of cybersecurity with a focus on mastering essential tools. This chapter equips you with hands-on knowledge of tools used in areas such as vulnerability assessment, penetration testing, and security monitoring. Gain practical insights into their applications, ensuring you're well-prepared to navigate the dynamic landscape of cybersecurity armed with the right instruments.

Chapter 6: Certifications as Milestones

Explore the significance of certifications as crucial milestones in your cybersecurity journey. This chapter provides insights into selecting and pursuing certifications that align with your career goals. From industry-recognized credentials to specialized certifications, learn how achieving these milestones not only validates your skills but also opens doors to new opportunities and career advancement within the cybersecurity realm.

Chapter 7: Gaining Practical Experience

Embark on the hands-on aspect of your cybersecurity journey. This chapter emphasizes the importance of practical experience, guiding you through real-world scenarios and exercises. From simulated environments to interactive challenges, discover how actively engaging with cybersecurity tasks enhances your skills and builds the practical foundation needed for success in the field.

Chapter 8: Networking and Mentoring

In this pivotal chapter, unlock the power of networking and mentorship in shaping your cybersecurity career. Explore strategies for building meaningful professional connections, both online and offline. Learn the art of mentorship—how it can accelerate your growth, provide guidance, and open doors to opportunities. Navigate the interconnected world of cybersecurity with a supportive network and valuable mentors by your side.

Chapter 9: Advancing Your Career

Transition from entry-level roles to strategic career advancement in this crucial chapter. Explore avenues for growth, including specialization, leadership roles, and contributing to the broader cybersecurity community. From staying updated on industry trends to becoming a thought leader, this chapter provides insights into sustaining a thriving and impactful cybersecurity career.

Chapter 10: Facing Challenges and Staying Resilient

Discover strategies for navigating challenges in the dynamic realm of cybersecurity. This chapter explores the resilience needed to overcome setbacks, adapt to evolving threats, and thrive in the face of adversity. Learn how to turn challenges into opportunities for growth, ensuring that you not only survive but flourish in your cybersecurity career journey.

Chapter 1: Introduction to Cyber World

Welcome to the Cybersecurity World

In an age dominated by technology, the digital realm has become an integral part of our daily lives, transforming the way we communicate, work, and live. However, this technological evolution has also brought about unprecedented challenges in the form of cyber threats, making cybersecurity more crucial than ever before. As an experienced cybersecurity professional, I am thrilled to guide you through the intricate and dynamic landscape of cybersecurity in this comprehensive guide - the "Cybersecurity Blueprint: A Strategic Guide to Launching Your Career."

The digital landscape is akin to a vast and interconnected universe, with its own set of rules, dangers, and opportunities. Just as pioneers explored uncharted territories, you are about to embark on a journey into the realm of cybersecurity, where every click, line of code, and network configuration matters. This book is designed to be your trusted companion, offering insights, strategies, and hands-on advice to help you navigate the complexities of cybersecurity and carve out a successful career in this rapidly evolving field.

The Growing Need for Cybersecurity Professionals

In recent years, we have witnessed an unprecedented surge in cyber threats, ranging from ransomware attacks on critical infrastructure to sophisticated phishing schemes targeting individuals and organizations alike. The frequency and severity of these incidents underscore the urgent need for skilled cybersecurity professionals who can defend against, mitigate, and respond to these ever-evolving threats.

The digital landscape is constantly evolving, and so are the tactics employed by cyber adversaries. As businesses, governments, and individuals become more reliant on technology, the attack surface for cyber threats widens, creating a demand for experts who can safeguard our digital future. Organizations across industries are waking up to the reality that cybersecurity is not just a technological investment but a strategic imperative for ensuring business continuity, protecting sensitive information, and maintaining the trust of stakeholders.

This growing need for cybersecurity professionals has created a unique and exciting opportunity for individuals like you to enter a field where your skills and knowledge can make a significant impact. Whether you are a seasoned IT professional looking to specialize or a newcomer fascinated by the world of cybersecurity, this guide will provide you with the tools and insights needed to not only meet the demands of the industry but to thrive in the face of evolving cyber threats.

Defining Your Path in Cybersecurity

As you stand at the threshold of a career in cybersecurity, it's crucial to understand that this field is not a one-size-fits-all endeavour. Cybersecurity encompasses a diverse array of specializations, each requiring specific skills, knowledge, and expertise. Just as a physician may choose to specialize in cardiology or neurology, a cybersecurity professional can find their niche in areas such as penetration testing, incident response, threat intelligence, or security architecture.

This book will guide you through the process of defining your path in cybersecurity, helping you identify your interests, strengths, and the specific areas of cybersecurity that align with your career goals. Whether you aspire to be the frontline defender, analysing and preventing cyber threats, or prefer the role of a strategist, designing robust security frameworks, the opportunities are vast and varied.

Understanding the fundamentals of cybersecurity is essential, and this guide will cover the core concepts that serve as the building blocks for any cybersecurity career. From mastering the basics of cryptography and network security to gaining proficiency in ethical hacking and security assessments, you will develop a solid foundation that will serve you well, regardless of your chosen specialization.

Beyond technical skills, effective communication, problem-solving, and a keen understanding of the business context are increasingly crucial in the world of cybersecurity. As organizations recognize the holistic nature of cybersecurity, professionals who can articulate complex security concepts to non-technical stakeholders and align security initiatives with business objectives are in high demand.

In the subsequent chapters, we will delve into the key pillars of cybersecurity, exploring topics such as risk management, compliance, and the latest advancements in cybersecurity technologies. Additionally, practical guidance on acquiring certifications, building a professional network, and staying abreast of industry trends will be provided to equip you with the tools needed to not only enter the cybersecurity field but to thrive and continuously evolve within it.

Conclusion:

In conclusion, the "Cybersecurity Blueprint" is more than just a guide; it is a roadmap for your journey into the dynamic and ever-evolving world of cybersecurity. Whether you are a recent graduate, a seasoned IT professional, or someone considering a career change, this book is designed to be your companion, offering insights, strategies, and practical advice to help you navigate the complexities of cybersecurity and build a successful and fulfilling career in this vital field. As you embark on this journey, remember that cybersecurity is not just a profession; it's a calling to protect and secure the digital future. Let's begin this exciting expedition into the heart of cybersecurity together.

Chapter 2: Assessing Your Skills and Interests

1. Self-Reflection and Skills Inventory

In the journey to becoming a proficient cybersecurity professional, a critical step is gaining clarity on your motivations and evaluating your current skill set. This process of self-reflection and skills inventory lays the foundation for a strategic and fulfilling career in the dynamic field of cybersecurity.

The Power of Self-Reflection

Before delving into the technical intricacies of cybersecurity, take the time for introspection. Ask yourself why you are drawn to this field. Is it the intellectual challenge, the ever-evolving threat landscape, or the desire to contribute to a safer digital world?

Key Reflection Points:

Motivations for Cybersecurity: Understanding what motivates you is essential. Whether it's the pursuit of justice, the thrill of ethical hacking, or the satisfaction of securing critical information, identifying these motivations will guide your career decisions.

Long-Term Vision: Envision where you see yourself in the cybersecurity landscape. Do you aspire to lead security initiatives, specialize in penetration testing, or perhaps contribute to policy and governance?

Conducting a Skills Inventory

Once your motivations are clarified, it's time to assess your skills. Cybersecurity demands a diverse skill set, both technical and soft. By identifying your strengths and weaknesses, you can tailor your learning journey to align with your career goals.

Comprehensive Skills Inventory

1. **Technical Proficiency:** List your technical skills, including programming languages, networking knowledge, and familiarity with operating systems. This inventory will serve as a baseline for understanding your technical aptitude.

2. **Soft Skills Assessment:** Effective communication, problem-solving, and teamwork are crucial in cybersecurity. Evaluate your soft skills to ensure a well-rounded skill set that extends beyond technical capabilities.

3. **Educational Background:** Assess your academic qualifications and certifications. Recognize areas where you may need additional education or training to strengthen your knowledge base.

Bridging the Skills Gap

Identifying gaps in your skill set is a normal part of this process. By comparing your current skills with the requirements of roles that align with your interests, you can formulate a plan to bridge these gaps and enhance your proficiency.

Strategies for Skills Enhancement:

Online Courses and Certifications: Explore reputable online platforms offering cybersecurity courses and certifications. These resources provide practical, hands-on experience and cover a broad range of cybersecurity topics.

Networking and Community Engagement: Join cybersecurity forums, attend conferences, and connect with professionals in the field. Networking not only expands your knowledge but also exposes you to different perspectives and opportunities.

Hands-On Practice: Set up a virtual lab environment to experiment with cybersecurity tools and techniques. Practical experience is a powerful teacher in cybersecurity.

2. Understanding Your Passion in Cybersecurity

Passion is the fuel that propels a cybersecurity professional through the challenges and triumphs of their career. Understanding your passion within the realm of cybersecurity is crucial for sustained motivation and success.

Identifying Your Driving Force

Dig deep into the aspects of cybersecurity that resonate with you. Is it the thrill of thwarting cyber threats, the intellectual satisfaction of solving intricate security puzzles, or the broader goal of contributing to a secure digital society?

Thought-Provoking Questions:

1. **Intrinsic Motivations:** Consider what aspects of cybersecurity provide you with a sense of purpose. Is it the pursuit of justice in the digital realm, the intellectual challenge, or the opportunity to innovate in security practices?

2. **Personal Values Alignment:** Reflect on how your personal values align with the ethical considerations in cybersecurity. Maintaining integrity and responsibility in your professional journey is crucial.

Navigating Cybersecurity Domains

Cybersecurity offers a diverse range of domains, each with its own set of challenges and opportunities. Connect your passion with specific cybersecurity domains to tailor your career path accordingly.

Exploring Domains:

1. **Ethical Hacking and Penetration Testing:** If the excitement of uncovering vulnerabilities and crafting secure systems intrigues you, ethical hacking and penetration testing might be your forte.

2. **Incident Response and Forensics:** If you are drawn to the detective work of investigating and mitigating security incidents, incident response and forensics could be a satisfying avenue.

3. **Governance, Risk, and Compliance (GRC):** For those interested in establishing and maintaining security policies and procedures, a career in GRC might align well with your passion.

3.Aligning Skills with Cybersecurity Roles

With a clear understanding of your passion and a comprehensive view of your skills, the next step is to align these with specific roles within the cybersecurity landscape. This ensures not only a fulfilling career but also maximizes your impact in the field.

Mapping Skills to Roles

Evaluate your skills and match them with the requirements of various cybersecurity roles. This process helps you identify roles where your unique skill set can shine, leading to a more purposeful and impactful career.

Skills-to-Roles Alignment:

1. **Penetration Testing and Ethical Hacking:** If you excel in identifying vulnerabilities and enjoy ethical hacking,

roles such as penetration tester or ethical hacker might be a natural fit.

2. **Security Analyst:** Strong analytical skills and attention to detail make you well-suited for a role as a security analyst. This role involves monitoring and responding to security incidents.

3. **Security Consultant:** If you possess excellent communication skills along with technical expertise, a role as a security consultant may be ideal. This involves advising organizations on security best practices.

Tailoring Your Career Path

With insights into your passion, skills, and their alignment with cybersecurity roles, you can now tailor your career path. This involves setting specific goals and crafting a roadmap for your professional development.

Customizing Your Journey:

1. **Short-Term and Long-Term Goals:** Define both short-term and long-term goals for your cybersecurity career. Short-term goals might include acquiring a specific certification, while long-term goals could involve reaching a leadership position in your chosen domain.

2. **Continuous Learning Plan:** Develop a plan for continuous learning. Cybersecurity is a field that evolves rapidly, and staying updated on emerging threats and technologies is crucial. Identify relevant conferences, webinars, and training programs to stay informed.

3. **Networking and Mentorship:** Actively engage in the cybersecurity community. Networking provides opportunities to learn from experienced professionals, discover potential career paths, and stay informed about

industry trends. Seek mentorship from seasoned individuals who can provide guidance based on their experiences.

Conclusion

Assessing your skills and interests in cybersecurity is a pivotal step toward a successful and fulfilling career. Self-reflection, understanding your passion, and aligning your skills with specific roles form the building blocks of your cybersecurity journey. Embrace the dynamic nature of the field, stay committed to continuous learning, and let your passion drive you toward becoming a proficient and impactful cybersecurity professional.

Chapter 3: Crafting Your Learning Path

Educational Options

In the rapidly evolving landscape of cybersecurity, a solid education is the cornerstone of a successful career. Crafting your learning path involves a strategic selection of educational options that align with your goals and pave the way for a rewarding journey in the field. This chapter will explore various educational avenues, empowering you to make informed decisions about your cybersecurity education.

Traditional Academic Paths

1. Bachelor's Degrees in Cybersecurity or Related Fields:

Pursuing a bachelor's degree in cybersecurity or a related field such as computer science, information technology, or computer engineering provides a comprehensive foundation. These programs cover a broad spectrum of topics, from network security to cryptography, and often include hands-on projects and internships.

2. Master's Degrees in Cybersecurity:

For those seeking advanced knowledge and specialization, a master's degree in cybersecurity is an excellent option. These programs delve deeper into specific areas such as ethical hacking, digital forensics, or security management. A master's degree can enhance your expertise and open doors to leadership roles.

Professional Certifications

3. Certified Information Systems Security Professional (CISSP):

Widely recognized in the industry, CISSP is a premier certification that covers various domains, including security and risk management, asset security, and security architecture. It is suitable for professionals aspiring to work in leadership or managerial roles.

4. CompTIA Security+ and Network+:

Entry-level certifications like CompTIA Security+ and Network+ are valuable for individuals starting their cybersecurity journey. They cover foundational concepts, preparing you for roles such as security analyst or network administrator.

5. Certified Ethical Hacker (CEH):

Aspiring ethical hackers can benefit from the CEH certification. This credential focuses on penetration testing techniques, ensuring that professionals can ethically identify and exploit vulnerabilities.

Online Learning Platforms

6. Coursera, edX, and Udacity:

Platforms like Coursera, edX, and Udacity offer a plethora of cybersecurity courses from top universities and institutions. These courses cover diverse topics, allowing you to tailor your learning based on your interests and career goals.

7. Cybersecurity Specializations on Coursera:

Platforms often feature specialized programs in cybersecurity, such as Google IT Support Professional Certificate and IBM Cybersecurity Analyst Professional Certificate. These hands-on courses provide practical skills and are recognized by industry leaders.

Cybersecurity Bootcamps

8. Full-Time or Part-Time Bootcamps:

Bootcamps provide an intensive and immersive learning experience. Full-time bootcamps are often immersive, while part-time options allow flexibility for working professionals. Look for reputable programs that offer real-world projects and networking opportunities.

9. Coding Bootcamps with a Focus on Cybersecurity:

Coding bootcamps, with a specific emphasis on cybersecurity, can be beneficial for those who want to develop hands-on technical skills quickly. These programs often cover programming languages, tools, and techniques used in the field.

On-the-Job Training and Certifications

10. Employer-Sponsored Training Programs:

Some employers offer training programs or tuition reimbursement for employees looking to advance their skills in cybersecurity. Explore opportunities within your current workplace to enhance your knowledge while gaining practical experience.

11. Vendor-Specific Certifications:

Many technology vendors offer certifications for their specific products and services. Examples include Cisco's CCNA Cyber Ops and Microsoft's Certified: Azure Security Engineer Associate. These certifications validate skills in using specific tools and technologies.

Continuous Learning Strategies

12. Engage in Capture the Flag (CTF) Competitions:

CTF competitions provide a gamified environment to practice and enhance cybersecurity skills. Participating in CTFs allows you to apply theoretical knowledge to real-world.

Specializations in Cybersecurity

In the intricate landscape of cybersecurity, specializing in a specific area is not only a strategic move but also a key factor in building a successful and fulfilling career. This chapter will delve into various specializations within cybersecurity, providing insights into the unique skills, knowledge, and opportunities each area presents. Understanding these specializations will empower you to make informed decisions as you craft your learning path in the realm of cybersecurity.

1. Ethical Hacking and Penetration Testing:

Specialization Overview:

Ethical hacking involves authorized attempts to breach the security of a system to identify vulnerabilities. Penetration testers simulate cyber-attacks to assess the strength of a system's defences.

Key Skills:

1. Proficiency in ethical hacking tools.
2. Understanding of common vulnerabilities and exploits.
3. Strong analytical and problem-solving skills.

Career Opportunities:

1. Penetration Tester
2. Ethical Hacker
3. Security Consultant

2. Incident Response and Forensics:

Specialization Overview:

Incident response specialists and digital forensics experts play a crucial role in investigating and mitigating security incidents. They analyse digital evidence to understand the nature of an attack and support legal proceedings.

Key Skills:

1. Cybercrime investigation techniques.
2. Digital forensics tools and methodologies.
3. Incident handling and response procedures.

Career Opportunities:

1. Incident Responder
2. Forensic Analyst
3. Cybersecurity Investigator

3. Security Architecture and Engineering:

Specialization Overview:

Security architects design and implement secure systems, networks, and applications. They create robust security frameworks to protect organizations from cyber threats.

Key Skills:

1. Secure system design principles.
2. Risk assessment and management.
3. Knowledge of security frameworks.

Career Opportunities:

1. Security Architect
2. Security Engineer
3. Systems Security Analyst

4. Governance, Risk, and Compliance (GRC):

Specialization Overview:

GRC specialists focus on establishing and maintaining security policies, ensuring regulatory compliance, and managing risk within an organization. They bridge the gap between technical and business aspects of cybersecurity.

Key Skills:

1. Compliance frameworks (e.g., GDPR, HIPAA).
2. Risk assessment and management.
3. Policy development and implementation.
4. Career Opportunities:
5. GRC Analyst
6. Compliance Officer
7. Risk Manager

5. Network Security:

Specialization Overview:

Network security specialists safeguard an organization's data by securing its network infrastructure. They implement measures to protect against unauthorized access, attacks, and data breaches.

Key Skills:

1. Firewalls and intrusion detection/prevention systems.
2. Network protocols and architecture.
3. VPNs and secure communication channels.
4. Career Opportunities:
5. Network Security Engineer
6. Network Security Administrator
7. Information Security Analyst

6. Cloud Security:

Specialization Overview:

With the increasing adoption of cloud technologies, cloud security specialists focus on securing cloud-based infrastructure, platforms, and applications. They address unique challenges associated with cloud computing.

Key Skills:

1. Cloud service providers' security models.

2. Identity and access management in the cloud.
3. Data encryption and privacy in the cloud.
4. Career Opportunities:
5. Cloud Security Architect
6. Cloud Security Engineer
7. Cloud Security Consultant

7. Mobile Security:

Specialization Overview:

Mobile security specialists focus on securing mobile devices, applications, and the associated infrastructure. With the proliferation of smartphones, this specialization addresses the unique challenges posed by mobile technology.

Key Skills:

1. Mobile application security testing.
2. Mobile device management.
3. Understanding of mobile operating systems.
4. Career Opportunities:
5. Mobile Security Analyst
6. Mobile Security Engineer
7. Mobile Security Consultant

8. IoT Security:

Specialization Overview:

As the Internet of Things (IoT) continues to expand, IoT security specialists focus on securing connected devices and the ecosystems they operate within. This involves addressing vulnerabilities unique to IoT environments.

Key Skills:

1. Understanding of IoT protocols.
2. Secure development practices for IoT devices.

3. IoT risk assessment and mitigation.

Career Opportunities:

1. IoT Security Specialist
2. IoT Security Consultant
3. Embedded Systems Security Engineer

9. Cryptography:

Specialization Overview:

Cryptographers work on developing and implementing cryptographic algorithms to secure data and communication. They play a vital role in ensuring the confidentiality and integrity of information.

Key Skills:

1. Mathematical foundations of cryptography.
2. Cryptographic protocols and algorithms.
3. Cryptanalysis and key management.
4. Career Opportunities:
5. Cryptographer
6. Cryptography Engineer
7. Security Researcher (Cryptography)

10. Threat Intelligence:

Specialization Overview:

Threat intelligence specialists focus on gathering and analysing information about cyber threats to help organizations make informed decisions. They provide valuable insights into the tactics and techniques used by adversaries.

Key Skills:

1. Cyber threat analysis.
2. Security information and event management (SIEM).
3. Threat intelligence platforms and tools.

Career Opportunities:

1. Threat Intelligence Analyst
2. Threat Hunter
3. Cyber Threat Researcher

Choosing Your Specialization

Selecting the right specialization is a crucial decision that will shape your career path in cybersecurity. Consider your interests, strengths, and long-term goals when making this choice. Specializations often intersect, allowing professionals to diversify their skill set over time. As you embark on your learning journey, keep in mind that the cybersecurity landscape is dynamic, and staying adaptable is key to long-term success in this ever-evolving field. Topic: Offensive Security

As we navigate the intricate world of cybersecurity, one specialization stands out for those who seek to proactively defend digital landscapes: Offensive Security. In this chapter, we'll delve into the realm of offensive security, exploring the skills, knowledge, and strategies required to become a proficient ethical hacker or penetration tester. Crafting your learning path in offensive security not only demands technical prowess but also a strategic and ethical mindset.

Understanding Offensive Security

Overview:

Offensive security revolves around simulating cyber-attacks to identify vulnerabilities, weaknesses, and potential entry points in a system. Professionals in this field, often referred to as ethical hackers or penetration testers, play a crucial role in fortifying digital defences by thinking like adversaries.

Key Skills:

Ethical Hacking Techniques:

1. Understanding common hacking methodologies.

2. Proficiency in ethical hacking tools (e.g., Metasploit, Burp Suite).
3. Exploiting vulnerabilities responsibly and ethically.

Penetration Testing:

1. Conducting comprehensive penetration tests.
2. Identifying and exploiting security weaknesses.
3. Providing actionable recommendations for mitigation.

Scripting and Coding:

1. Proficiency in scripting languages (e.g., Python, Bash).
2. Creating custom exploits and tools.
3. Automating repetitive tasks in ethical hacking processes.

Networking and Systems Knowledge:

1. In-depth understanding of network protocols and architectures.
2. Familiarity with various operating systems (Windows, Linux, Unix).
3. Analyzing and manipulating network traffic.
4. Crafting Your Offensive Security Learning Path

1. Foundational Knowledge:

Begin by establishing a solid foundation in cybersecurity concepts, networking, and systems. Familiarize yourself with common security vulnerabilities, attack vectors, and defence mechanisms. Earning certifications like CompTIA Security+ is a recommended starting point.

2. Hands-On Labs and Capture the Flag (CTF) Challenges:

Engage in practical, hands-on labs and CTF challenges to apply theoretical knowledge in real-world scenarios. Platforms like Hack the Box, TryHackMe, and OverTheWire offer a variety of challenges that cater to different skill levels.

3. Ethical Hacking Certifications:

1. Acquire industry-recognized certifications that validate your skills in ethical hacking and penetration testing. Certifications provide a structured learning path and enhance your credibility in the field. Key certifications include:
2. Certified Ethical Hacker (CEH): Covers a broad range of ethical hacking techniques and tools.
3. Offensive Security Certified Professional (OSCP): A hands-on certification that involves completing practical penetration testing challenges.
4. eLearnSecurity Certified Professional Penetration Tester (eCPPT): Focuses on practical skills through simulated environments.

4. Advanced Techniques and Specializations:

1. Delve into advanced offensive security techniques and specializations to broaden your skill set.
2. Web Application Penetration Testing: Focus on vulnerabilities specific to web applications using tools like Burp Suite and OWASP Zap.
3. Wireless Network Penetration Testing: Explore security challenges associated with wireless networks and protocols.
4. Hardware Hacking and IoT Security: Learn to assess the security of hardware devices and Internet of Things (IoT) ecosystems.

5. Practical Experience:

Gain practical experience through internships, freelance projects, or bug bounty programs. Real-world experience is invaluable in developing the problem-solving skills essential for an offensive security professional.

6. Continuous Learning and Professional Development:

Offensive security is a dynamic field that constantly evolves. Stay updated on emerging threats, new hacking techniques, and evolving security measures. Attend conferences, webinars, and workshops to connect with the broader cybersecurity community.

7. Build a Professional Network:

Connect with professionals in offensive security through online forums, social media, and industry events. Networking provides opportunities to share knowledge, seek advice, and explore potential collaborations.

Ethical Considerations in Offensive Security

As you embark on the journey of offensive security, it's crucial to emphasize the ethical aspect of your work. Ethical hackers and penetration testers have a responsibility to conduct their activities within legal and ethical boundaries. Some key ethical considerations include:

Authorization: Ensure you have explicit authorization before conducting any penetration testing or ethical hacking activities. Unauthorized testing can lead to legal consequences.

Data Privacy: Respect the privacy of individuals and organizations. Avoid collecting, storing, or disseminating sensitive information without proper consent.

Documentation: Thoroughly document your activities, findings, and recommendations. Clear documentation is essential for transparent communication with stakeholders.

Responsible Disclosure: If you discover vulnerabilities during your testing, follow responsible disclosure practices. Notify the affected parties and provide them with sufficient time to address the issues before public disclosure.

Continuous Professional Development: Stay informed about the latest ethical hacking guidelines, legal frameworks, and industry best practices. Engage in continuous learning to enhance your ethical hacking skills and knowledge.

Advancing Your Offensive Security Career

As you accumulate experience and expertise in offensive security, consider the following strategies to advance your career:

Specialize Further: Explore niche areas within offensive security, such as red teaming, malware analysis, or advanced exploitation techniques.

Achieve Advanced Certifications: Pursue advanced certifications that demonstrate your expertise in specific offensive security domains. Examples include the Offensive Security Certified Expert (OSCE) and the Certified Expert Penetration Tester (CEPT).

Mentorship and Knowledge Sharing: Engage in mentorship relationships to guide and support aspiring professionals. Additionally, contribute to the community by sharing your knowledge through blog posts, presentations, or workshops.

Leadership Roles: As you gain experience, consider transitioning into leadership roles within offensive security teams. Leadership positions may involve overseeing penetration testing projects, managing red team engagements, or leading security research initiatives.

Continuous Innovation: Stay at the forefront of offensive security by exploring innovative techniques, tools, and methodologies. Actively contribute to the advancement of offensive security practices.

In conclusion, offensive security is a dynamic and challenging field that demands a unique set of skills and a commitment to ethical practices. By crafting a learning path that combines foundational knowledge, hands-on experience, and continuous professional development, you can position yourself as a proficient and responsible offensive security professional. Embrace the journey, stay curious, and contribute to the ongoing evolution of cybersecurity.

Defensive Security

In the ever-evolving landscape of cybersecurity, defensive security plays a pivotal role in safeguarding organizations from cyber threats. This chapter explores the nuances of defensive security, guiding aspiring professionals on the skills, strategies, and learning paths necessary to build a successful career in defending digital infrastructures.

Understanding Defensive Security

Overview:

Defensive security focuses on protecting systems, networks, and data from unauthorized access, cyber-attacks, and security breaches. Professionals in this field, often known as cybersecurity defenders or security analysts, work diligently to establish robust security postures and respond effectively to potential threats.

Key Skills:

Security Monitoring and Incident Response:

1. Utilizing security information and event management (SIEM) tools.
2. Analyzing logs and alerts to detect and respond to security incidents.
3. Conducting incident response and forensic investigations.

Network Security:

1. Configuring and managing firewalls and intrusion detection/prevention systems.
2. Implementing secure network architectures and protocols.
3. Monitoring network traffic for anomalies and potential threats.

Endpoint Security:

1. Deploying and managing antivirus and endpoint protection solutions.
2. Conducting vulnerability assessments and patch management.
3. Implementing endpoint detection and response (EDR) solutions.

Security Policy and Compliance:

1. Developing and enforcing security policies and procedures.
2. Ensuring compliance with industry regulations and standards.
3. Conducting security audits and risk assessments.

Crafting Your Defensive Security Learning Path

1. Foundational Knowledge:

Begin your defensive security journey by establishing a solid foundation in cybersecurity fundamentals. Understand basic concepts such as encryption, authentication, and security protocols. Earning certifications like CompTIA Security+ can provide a strong starting point.

2. Networking and Systems Proficiency:

Develop a deep understanding of networking and systems administration. Familiarize yourself with the architecture of operating systems (Windows, Linux, Unix) and grasp how data flows across networks. Certifications like CompTIA Network+ and Microsoft Certified: Azure Fundamentals can enhance your networking knowledge.

3. Security Certifications:

Earn industry-recognized certifications that validate your expertise in defensive security. Key certifications include:

Certified Information Systems Security Professional (CISSP): Covers a wide range of security domains, emphasizing managerial and strategic aspects.

CompTIA Security+: Focuses on foundational cybersecurity skills with an emphasis on practical applications.

Certified Information Security Manager (CISM): Designed for individuals involved in managing information security systems.

4. Hands-On Training and Simulations:

Engage in hands-on training exercises and simulations to apply theoretical knowledge to real-world scenarios. Platforms like CyberRange and Microsoft Cybersecurity Learning Paths offer practical, scenario-based learning experiences.

5. Security Operations Center (SOC) Experience:

Gain practical experience by working in a Security Operations Center (SOC) environment. SOC analysts are at the forefront of defending organizations against cyber threats. Practical exposure to security monitoring, incident response, and threat intelligence is invaluable.

6. Advanced Defensive Techniques:

Delve into advanced defensive techniques and tools to enhance your skill set:

Threat Hunting: Proactively searching for potential security threats within an environment.

Security Automation and Orchestration: Implementing automated responses to security incidents.

Cloud Security: Understanding security principles and best practices in cloud environments.

7. Continuous Learning and Skill Enhancement:

Defensive security is a dynamic field that requires staying ahead of evolving threats. Engage in continuous learning through webinars, conferences, and training programs. Stay informed about emerging technologies and threat landscapes.

8. Cybersecurity Frameworks and Standards:

Understand and implement cybersecurity frameworks and standards that guide best practices. Familiarize yourself with frameworks such as NIST Cybersecurity Framework, ISO/IEC 27001, and CIS Critical Security Controls.

Ethical Considerations in Defensive Security

As a defender, ethical considerations are paramount in ensuring the responsible and lawful execution of defensive security practices. Key ethical considerations include:

Respect for Privacy:

1. Uphold individuals' privacy rights by ensuring that defensive measures do not infringe on personal freedoms.
2. Avoid unnecessary data collection and handling.

Transparency and Accountability:

1. Maintain transparency in security practices and communicate openly with stakeholders.
2. Take responsibility for the effectiveness of security measures and incident responses.

Legal and Regulatory Compliance:

1. Adhere to legal and regulatory requirements governing defensive security practices.
2. Stay informed about changes in legislation that may impact defensive security operations.

Ethical Hacking and Testing:

1. If conducting ethical hacking or testing, ensure proper authorization is obtained.

2. Report findings responsibly and adhere to disclosure guidelines.

Balancing Security and Usability:

1. Strive to implement security measures without compromising the usability and functionality of systems.
2. Seek a balance that enhances security without hindering legitimate user activities.

Advancing Your Defensive Security Career

As you progress in your defensive security career, consider the following strategies for professional advancement:

Specialize in Specific Domains:

1. Focus on specific domains within defensive security, such as incident response, threat intelligence, or cloud security.
2. Specialization can open doors to more advanced and specialized roles.

Management and Leadership Roles:

1. Explore managerial and leadership roles within cybersecurity, such as Security Operations Manager or Chief Information Security Officer (CISO).
2. Leadership roles involve strategic planning, policy development, and overseeing security programs.

Industry Involvement and Networking:

1. Engage with the cybersecurity community through industry events, conferences, and online forums.
2. Networking can lead to valuable connections, knowledge sharing, and potential career opportunities.

Continuous Certification and Training:

1. Pursue advanced certifications as you gain experience, such as Certified Information Systems Security Professional (CISSP) or Certified Information Security Manager (CISM).

2. Stay updated on the latest developments in defensive security through continuous training.

Contributions to Knowledge Sharing:

1. Contribute to the cybersecurity community by sharing your knowledge through blogs, articles, or presentations.
2. Participate in mentoring programs to guide aspiring professionals.

Conclusion

Defensive security is a critical and dynamic field that requires a combination of technical proficiency, strategic thinking, and ethical considerations. By crafting a learning path that emphasizes foundational knowledge, hands-on experience, and continuous skill enhancement, you can position yourself as a skilled defender in the ever-evolving landscape of cybersecurity. Embrace the challenges, stay curious, and contribute to the ongoing mission of safeguarding digital assets from cyber threats.

Governance, Risk Management, and Compliance (GRC)

In the intricate tapestry of cybersecurity, mastering the principles of Governance, Risk Management, and Compliance (GRC) is akin to becoming the architect of an organization's cyber resilience. This chapter delves into the realm of GRC, offering insights into the skills, strategies, and learning paths essential for those aspiring to navigate the complexities of governing, managing risks, and ensuring compliance within the cybersecurity landscape.

Understanding GRC in Cybersecurity

Overview:

Governance, Risk Management, and Compliance (GRC) form the bedrock of effective cybersecurity strategy. These three interrelated components work in harmony to ensure that an organization's cybersecurity measures align with business objectives, mitigate potential risks, and comply with industry regulations and standards.

Key Skills:

Policy Development and Implementation:

1. Crafting comprehensive cybersecurity policies aligned with organizational objectives.
2. Ensuring effective communication and adherence to policies throughout the organization.

Risk Assessment and Mitigation:

1. Identifying and assessing cybersecurity risks that could impact the organization.
2. Developing risk mitigation strategies and contingency plans.

Compliance Management:

1. Ensuring adherence to relevant cybersecurity laws, regulations, and industry standards.
2. Conducting regular compliance audits and assessments.

Security Governance:

1. Establishing and maintaining a robust cybersecurity governance framework.
2. Defining roles, responsibilities, and accountability for cybersecurity initiatives.

Crafting Your GRC Learning Path

1. Foundational Knowledge:

Begin by building a solid foundation in cybersecurity principles, policies, and risk management. Understand the core concepts of confidentiality, integrity, and availability (CIA), as well as the legal and regulatory landscape. Certifications like CompTIA Security+ provide an excellent starting point for foundational knowledge.

2. Risk Management Certifications:

Dive deeper into risk management by obtaining certifications that focus on assessing and mitigating cybersecurity risks. Key certifications include:

Certified Information Systems Risk Professional (CRISC): Emphasizes risk management and control implementation.

Risk Management Professional (PMI-RMP): Focuses on risk management within the context of project management.

3. Compliance Certifications:

Explore certifications that specifically address compliance management and regulatory frameworks. Relevant certifications include:

Certified Information Systems Auditor (CISA): Focuses on auditing, control, and security of information systems.

Certified in Risk and Information Systems Control (CRISC): Covers risk identification, assessment, and response.

4. Legal and Regulatory Knowledge:

Develop a thorough understanding of cybersecurity laws, regulations, and industry standards applicable to your region and industry. Stay informed about changes and updates in the legal landscape, especially those related to data protection and privacy.

5. Security Governance Frameworks:

Familiarize yourself with established security governance frameworks that guide organizational cybersecurity practices. Examples include:

NIST Cybersecurity Framework: Provides a risk-based approach to managing cybersecurity.

ISO/IEC 27001: An international standard for information security management systems.

6. Business Acumen:

Develop business acumen to align cybersecurity initiatives with organizational goals and objectives. Understand the organization's structure, processes, and industry context. This knowledge is crucial for effective GRC implementation.

7. Continuous Learning and Professional Development:

Stay abreast of emerging trends, technologies, and changes in the regulatory environment. Attend GRC-focused conferences, webinars, and training sessions to enhance your knowledge and network with professionals in the field.

Ethical Considerations in GRC

Given the strategic nature of GRC in cybersecurity, ethical considerations are paramount. Ethical conduct is crucial when dealing with governance, risk management, and compliance initiatives. Key ethical considerations include:

Transparent Communication:

1. Maintain transparent communication with stakeholders regarding cybersecurity policies, risks, and compliance efforts.
2. Disclose relevant information without compromising confidentiality.

Fair and Equitable Practices:

1. Ensure that governance, risk management, and compliance practices are applied consistently and fairly across the organization.
2. Avoid favouritism or bias in decision-making processes.

Data Privacy and Protection:

1. Uphold the principles of data privacy and protection when managing risk and compliance efforts.
2. Safeguard sensitive information and adhere to data protection laws.

Adherence to Legal and Regulatory Requirements:

1. Comply with all applicable legal and regulatory requirements related to cybersecurity governance, risk management, and compliance.
2. Stay informed about changes in legislation that may impact GRC practices.

Responsible Reporting and Documentation:

1. Document GRC activities accurately and comprehensively.
2. Report risks and compliance status responsibly, providing stakeholders with the information needed for informed decision-making.

Advancing Your GRC Career

As you progress in your GRC career, consider the following strategies for professional advancement:

Specialization in Specific GRC Domains:

1. Focus on specific areas within GRC, such as compliance management, risk analysis, or security governance.
2. Specialization allows for in-depth expertise in a particular facet of GRC.

Advanced Certifications:

Pursue advanced certifications in GRC to demonstrate specialized knowledge and expertise. Examples include the Certified Information Systems Security Professional (CISSP) and Certified Information Security Manager (CISM) certifications.

Leadership Roles:

1. Aim for leadership roles within GRC departments, such as Chief Information Security Officer (CISO) or Director of GRC.
2. Leadership positions involve strategic planning, policy development, and overseeing the execution of GRC programs.

Industry Involvement and Networking:

1. Engage with GRC professionals and organizations through industry events, conferences, and online forums.
2. Networking provides opportunities for knowledge sharing, mentorship, and career growth.

Continuous Contribution to GRC Knowledge:

1. Contribute to the broader GRC community by sharing your knowledge through articles, presentations, or workshops.
2. Participate in mentorship programs to guide and support emerging professionals in GRC.

Conclusion

Governance, Risk Management, and Compliance (GRC) in cybersecurity form the cornerstone of a resilient and well-protected digital infrastructure. By crafting a learning path that encompasses foundational knowledge, specialized certifications, and a commitment to ethical practices, you can position yourself as a strategic GRC professional. Embrace the challenges, stay attuned to industry developments, and contribute to the ongoing mission of securing organizations against cyber threats.

Chapter 4: Building a Solid Foundation

Networking Essentials

In the dynamic realm of cybersecurity, establishing a strong foundation in networking is akin to laying the groundwork for a resilient and secure digital infrastructure. This chapter explores the critical importance of Networking Essentials, guiding aspiring cybersecurity professionals on the skills, strategies, and learning paths necessary to navigate the intricacies of networking in the cyber landscape.

Understanding Networking Essentials

Overview:

Networking forms the backbone of the digital world, connecting devices, systems, and users across the globe. In cybersecurity, a profound understanding of networking is fundamental, as it underpins various security measures and strategies. Networking essentials encompass a range of topics, from the basics of protocols and communication to more advanced concepts like network security and architecture.

Key Skills:

Protocols and Communication:

1. Understanding the fundamentals of networking protocols (TCP/IP, UDP).
2. Grasping how devices communicate over a network.

Network Topologies and Architectures:

1. Knowledge of different network topologies (star, bus, mesh).
2. Understanding network architectures, including local area networks (LANs) and wide area networks (WANs).

Subnetting and IP Addressing:

1. Proficiency in subnetting to efficiently allocate IP addresses.
2. Understanding IPv4 and IPv6 addressing schemes.

Routing and Switching:

1. Grasping the principles of routing and switching.
2. Configuring and managing network routers and switches.

Network Security Fundamentals:

1. Awareness of basic network security measures.
2. Understanding the role of firewalls, intrusion detection systems (IDS), and virtual private networks (VPNs).

Crafting Your Networking Essentials Learning Path

1. Foundational Knowledge:

Begin your journey by establishing a solid foundation in networking fundamentals. Familiarize yourself with basic concepts such as data encapsulation, the OSI model, and the TCP/IP protocol suite. Books like "Computer Networking: Principles, Protocols and Practice" by Olivier Bonaventure can provide comprehensive insights into networking basics.

2. Online Networking Courses:

Enrol in online courses that cover networking essentials. Platforms like Coursera, edX, and LinkedIn Learning offer courses ranging from beginner to advanced levels. Look for courses that include hands-on labs and real-world scenarios to reinforce theoretical knowledge.

3. Networking Certifications:

Obtain industry-recognized certifications to validate your networking skills. Key certifications include:

CompTIA Network+: Covers essential networking concepts and is suitable for beginners.

Cisco Certified Network Associate (CCNA): Focuses on more advanced topics, including routing, switching, and network security.

Juniper Networks Certified Associate (JNCIA): Provides a solid understanding of Juniper networking technologies.

4. Practical Labs and Simulations:

Set up practical labs to apply theoretical knowledge in a hands-on environment. Tools like Packet Tracer, GNS3, or Cisco's VIRL allow you to simulate network configurations and scenarios. Engaging in labs enhances your troubleshooting and configuration skills.

5. Networking Books and Resources:

Read authoritative books on networking to deepen your understanding. Explore resources like "Network Warrior" by Gary A. Donahue or "TCP/IP Illustrated" by Kevin R. Fall and W. Richard Stevens. These resources provide practical insights and real-world examples.

6. Networking Hardware Familiarity:

Gain hands-on experience with networking hardware, including routers, switches, and access points. Setting up a home lab or volunteering for networking projects allows you to interact with physical devices, reinforcing your knowledge.

7. Join Networking Communities:

Participate in online forums, social media groups, and networking communities. Platforms like Reddit (e.g., r/networking) and Cisco Community provide spaces for networking professionals to share knowledge, seek advice, and discuss industry trends.

Ethical Considerations in Networking

Given the critical role of networking in cybersecurity, ethical considerations are paramount. Networking professionals often deal with sensitive information and have the responsibility to maintain ethical standards. Key ethical considerations include:

Respect for Privacy:

1. Protect user privacy by implementing secure communication channels and encryption.
2. Avoid unauthorized monitoring or interception of sensitive data.

Integrity in Network Administration:

1. Maintain the integrity of network configurations and data.
2. Refrain from unauthorized modifications that could compromise the stability or security of the network.

Transparent Communication:

1. Clearly communicate network policies, configurations, and changes to stakeholders.
2. Provide adequate notice for planned network maintenance or updates.

Responsible Disclosure:

1. If identifying vulnerabilities in network configurations, follow responsible disclosure practices.
2. Notify relevant parties promptly and provide them with an opportunity to address the issues.

Ethical Hacking Practices:

1. If engaging in ethical hacking or penetration testing, ensure proper authorization is obtained.
2. Adhere to guidelines and legal frameworks governing ethical hacking practices.

Advancing Your Networking Career

As you progress in your networking career, consider the following strategies for professional advancement:

Specialization in Network Security:

1. Focus on network security as a specialization, gaining expertise in firewalls, intrusion prevention systems (IPS), and secure network design.
2. Certifications such as the Certified Information Systems Security Professional (CISSP) can complement your networking skills with a security focus.

Advanced Certifications:

Pursue advanced networking certifications to demonstrate specialized knowledge. Examples include the Cisco Certified Internetwork Expert (CCIE) or Juniper Networks Certified Internet Associate (JNCIA).

Networking Architecture and Design:

1. Develop expertise in network architecture and design principles.
2. Consider certifications or training programs that focus on designing scalable and secure networks.

Leadership Roles:

1. Aim for leadership roles within networking teams or IT departments.
2. Leadership positions involve overseeing network projects, strategic planning, and coordinating with other departments.

Continuous Learning and Industry Involvement:

1. Stay updated on emerging networking technologies, protocols, and industry trends.
2. Attend conferences, webinars, and workshops to network with professionals and stay informed about the latest developments.

Conclusion

Networking essentials are the cornerstone of a successful career in cybersecurity. By crafting a learning path that encompasses foundational knowledge, hands-on experience, and a commitment to ethical practices, you can position yourself as a skilled networking professional. Embrace the journey, stay curious, and contribute to the seamless connectivity and security of the digital world.

TCP/IP Fundamentals

In the intricate landscape of cybersecurity, understanding the fundamentals of TCP/IP is akin to deciphering the language of the digital world. This chapter delves into the critical importance of TCP/IP fundamentals, providing aspiring cybersecurity professionals with insights into the skills, strategies, and learning paths necessary to navigate the complexities of this foundational networking protocol.

Understanding TCP/IP Fundamentals

Overview:

Transmission Control Protocol/Internet Protocol (TCP/IP) is the backbone of modern networking, serving as the primary communication protocol for the internet and intranets. A comprehensive grasp of TCP/IP fundamentals is essential for cybersecurity professionals, as it forms the basis for network communication, security protocols, and data transmission.

Key Skills:

Understanding the OSI Model:

1. Grasping the layers of the OSI model and their relevance to TCP/IP.
2. Identifying the role of each OSI layer in the communication process.

TCP/IP Protocol Suite:

1. Familiarity with the key protocols within the TCP/IP suite, including IP, TCP, UDP, ICMP, and ARP.
2. Understanding the functions and responsibilities of each protocol.

IP Addressing and Subnetting:

1. Mastery of IPv4 and IPv6 addressing schemes.
2. Proficiency in subnetting to efficiently allocate IP addresses.

Routing and Switching Concepts:

1. Understanding the principles of routing and switching within a TCP/IP network.
2. Configuring and managing network routers and switches.

Packet Analysis:

1. Ability to analyze network packets using tools like Wireshark.
2. Identifying and troubleshooting network issues through packet analysis.

Crafting Your TCP/IP Fundamentals Learning Path

1. Foundational Knowledge:

Begin by establishing a solid foundation in networking basics, including the OSI model and the fundamentals of data communication.

Familiarize yourself with the structure and purpose of each OSI layer, as well as the concept of encapsulation. Books like "TCP/IP Illustrated" by Kevin R. Fall and W. Richard Stevens provide in-depth insights into TCP/IP fundamentals.

2. Online Courses on TCP/IP:

Enrol in online courses that specifically cover TCP/IP fundamentals. Platforms like Coursera, edX, and Pluralsight offer courses designed to cater to various skill levels. Look for courses that include practical demonstrations and hands-on labs to reinforce theoretical concepts.

3. Practical Labs and Simulations:

Set up practical labs or use simulation tools to apply TCP/IP concepts in a hands-on environment. Tools like Cisco Packet Tracer, GNS3, or even virtualization platforms with networking capabilities allow you to simulate and experiment with TCP/IP configurations.

4. Networking Certifications:

Obtain certifications that validate your proficiency in TCP/IP and networking. Key certifications include:

CompTIA Network+: Covers TCP/IP fundamentals and serves as a foundational networking certification.

Cisco Certified Network Associate (CCNA): Focuses on networking concepts, including TCP/IP, routing, and switching.

5. Books on TCP/IP:

Read authoritative books on TCP/IP to gain deeper insights into its workings. Besides "TCP/IP Illustrated," consider resources like "TCP/IP Guide" by Charles M. Kozierok or "Internetworking with TCP/IP" by Douglas E. Comer. These resources provide detailed explanations and practical examples.

6. Hands-On Configuration and Troubleshooting:

Practice configuring TCP/IP settings on networking devices, such as routers and switches. Experiment with different IP addressing schemes, subnetting, and routing configurations. Develop the ability to troubleshoot TCP/IP-related issues effectively.

7. Networking Forums and Communities:

Engage in networking forums and communities to discuss TCP/IP concepts with other professionals. Platforms like Stack Exchange Network Engineering or Cisco Community provide spaces for asking questions, sharing knowledge, and gaining insights from experienced practitioners.

Ethical Considerations in TCP/IP

Given the foundational nature of TCP/IP in networking and cybersecurity, ethical considerations are paramount. Ethical conduct is essential when dealing with network protocols and communication. Key ethical considerations include:

Responsible Packet Analysis:

1. When performing packet analysis, respect privacy and avoid capturing sensitive information.
2. Use packet analysis tools responsibly and adhere to legal and ethical guidelines.

Transparent Communication:

1. Clearly communicate network configurations and changes, especially when implementing TCP/IP-related modifications.
2. Provide adequate notice for planned network maintenance or updates.

Data Privacy in IP Addressing:

1. Safeguard the privacy of individuals by implementing secure IP addressing and subnetting practices.
2. Avoid unnecessary collection or exposure of private IP addresses.

Responsible Use of Network Tools:

1. Use network tools and utilities responsibly, ensuring that they are employed for legitimate and authorized purposes.
2. Avoid any activities that could lead to network disruptions or unauthorized access.

Advancing Your TCP/IP Fundamentals Knowledge

As you progress in your TCP/IP fundamentals knowledge, consider the following strategies for professional advancement:

Advanced TCP/IP Certifications:

Pursue advanced certifications that focus specifically on TCP/IP and networking protocols. Advanced certifications may include Cisco Certified Internetwork Expert (CCIE) or specialized certifications offered by networking vendors.

Specialization in Network Security:

Explore specializations within networking that focus on security aspects of TCP/IP, such as securing communication through encryption and implementing secure network architectures.

Protocol Analysis and Troubleshooting Mastery:

1. Develop expertise in protocol analysis tools and techniques.
2. Master the art of troubleshooting TCP/IP-related issues efficiently.

Contributions to Networking Community:

1. Share your knowledge and experiences in TCP/IP by contributing to networking communities.
2. Participate in discussions, write blog posts, or conduct workshops to help others deepen their understanding.

Stay Updated on TCP/IP Developments:

1. Stay informed about developments in TCP/IP and networking technologies.
2. Attend conferences, webinars, and workshops focused on networking to keep abreast of the latest trends and advancements.

Conclusion

TCP/IP fundamentals serve as the bedrock of networking and cybersecurity. By crafting a learning path that encompasses foundational knowledge, hands-on experience, and a commitment to ethical practices, you can position yourself as a proficient professional in the intricate world of TCP/IP. Embrace the journey, stay curious, and contribute to the seamless communication and security of the digital landscape.

Subnetting and Routing

In the multifaceted field of cybersecurity, mastering the intricacies of subnetting and routing is akin to becoming a proficient navigator in the digital landscape. This chapter delves into the critical importance of Subnetting and Routing, providing aspiring cybersecurity professionals with insights into the skills, strategies, and learning paths necessary to unravel the complexities of these essential networking concepts.

Understanding Subnetting and Routing

Overview: Subnetting and routing are foundational elements of networking, playing a crucial role in designing efficient and secure network architectures. Subnetting involves dividing an IP network into smaller, more manageable sub-networks, while routing deals with the process of directing data packets between different networks. A deep understanding of these concepts is essential for cybersecurity professionals, as they form the basis for creating robust and scalable network infrastructures.

Key Skills:

IP Subnetting:

1. Proficiency in subnetting IPv4 and IPv6 addresses.
2. Understanding the purpose and benefits of subnetting in network design.

Subnet Masking:

3. Knowledge of subnet mask notation and its application in defining subnets.
4. Calculating subnet masks based on network requirements.

Variable Length Subnet Masking (VLSM):

5. Mastery of Variable Length Subnet Masking for optimizing IP address allocation.
6. Implementing VLSM to accommodate varying subnet sizes within a network.

Routing Protocols:

7. Understanding dynamic and static routing protocols.
8. Configuring and managing routers to enable effective packet routing.

Routing Tables:

9. Interpretation and manipulation of routing tables.
10. Configuring routing tables to influence traffic flow within a network.

Crafting Your Subnetting and Routing Learning Path

1. Foundational Networking Knowledge:

Begin by solidifying your understanding of basic networking concepts, including IP addressing, the OSI model, and the fundamentals of data communication. Familiarize yourself with the role of routers in directing data between networks.

2. Online Courses on Subnetting and Routing:

Enrol in online courses specifically tailored to cover subnetting and routing. Platforms like Cisco Networking Academy, Udemy, and Pluralsight offer courses ranging from beginner to advanced levels. Look for courses that include practical exercises and real-world scenarios.

3. Practical Labs and Simulations:

Set up practical labs or leverage simulation tools to gain hands-on experience with subnetting and routing configurations. Tools like Packet Tracer, GNS3, or Cisco VIRL allow you to simulate network scenarios and experiment with different subnetting and routing configurations.

4. Networking Certifications:

Obtain certifications that validate your skills in subnetting and routing. Key certifications include:

Cisco Certified Network Associate (CCNA): Covers routing and switching fundamentals, making it an ideal certification for aspiring network professionals.

CompTIA Network+: Includes topics on subnetting and routing, providing a solid foundation for networking.

5. Books on Subnetting and Routing:

Read authoritative books dedicated to subnetting and routing to deepen your understanding. Resources like "Routing TCP/IP" by Jeff Doyle and Jennifer DeHaven Carroll or "TCP/IP Guide" by Charles M. Kozierok provide comprehensive insights into routing protocols and subnetting practices.

6. Hands-On Configuration and Troubleshooting:

Engage in hands-on exercises to configure routers, implement subnetting, and troubleshoot network issues related to routing. Practical experience is invaluable in cementing theoretical knowledge.

7. Networking Forums and Communities:

Participate in online forums and communities dedicated to networking. Platforms like Cisco Community or Reddit's r/networking provide spaces for networking professionals to discuss subnetting, routing, and share experiences.

Ethical Considerations in Subnetting and Routing

Given the critical role of subnetting and routing in network design and security, ethical considerations are paramount. Ethical conduct is essential when dealing with network configurations and traffic routing. Key ethical considerations include:

Transparent Communication:

Clearly communicate changes to subnetting and routing configurations, especially those that could impact network traffic.

Provide advance notice for planned maintenance or updates that may affect network connectivity.

Data Privacy in Routing:

1. Implement secure routing practices to safeguard the privacy and integrity of data in transit.
2. Avoid routing configurations that could compromise the confidentiality of sensitive information.

Responsible Use of Routing Protocols:

1. Configure and use routing protocols responsibly, ensuring that they align with the organization's security policies.
2. Avoid configurations that could lead to network instability or unauthorized access.

Documentation and Change Control:

1. Maintain accurate documentation of subnetting and routing configurations.
2. Adhere to change control processes to ensure that all modifications are authorized and well-documented.

Advancing Your Subnetting and Routing Knowledge

As you progress in your understanding of subnetting and routing, consider the following strategies for professional advancement:

Advanced Routing Certifications:

Pursue advanced certifications that focus specifically on routing technologies. Certifications such as the Cisco Certified Internetwork Expert (CCIE) or Juniper Networks Certified Internet Professional (JNCIP) provide in-depth knowledge.

Specialization in Network Design:

Explore specializations within network design, focusing on optimizing subnetting practices and implementing efficient routing strategies.

Network Automation and Orchestration:

1. Gain skills in network automation tools and orchestration platforms.
2. Automate routine subnetting and routing tasks to enhance efficiency and reduce the risk of human error.

Contributions to Networking Community:

1. Share your expertise with the networking community by contributing to forums, blogs, or presenting at conferences.
2. Mentor aspiring professionals in subnetting and routing to foster knowledge sharing.

Continuous Learning and Industry Involvement:

1. Stay updated on emerging technologies and advancements in subnetting and routing.
2. Attend conferences, webinars, and workshops focused on networking to stay abreast of the latest trends.

Conclusion

Subnetting and routing are fundamental skills that empower cybersecurity professionals to design, optimize, and secure network infrastructures. By crafting a learning path that encompasses foundational knowledge, practical experience, and ethical considerations, you can position yourself as a proficient navigator in the ever-evolving digital landscape. Embrace the challenges, stay curious, and contribute to the seamless and secure flow of data within interconnected networks.

Operating System Proficiency

In the dynamic world of cybersecurity, mastering operating systems is akin to understanding the very fabric upon which digital landscapes are built. This chapter explores the critical importance of

Operating System Proficiency, providing aspiring cybersecurity professionals with insights into the skills, strategies, and learning paths necessary to navigate the complexities of various operating systems.

Understanding Operating System Proficiency

Overview: Operating systems serve as the foundation for computing devices, providing a platform for applications and enabling communication between hardware and software components. Proficiency in operating systems is a cornerstone of cybersecurity, as it empowers professionals to secure, configure, and analyze the security posture of systems across diverse environments.

Key Skills:

Security Configuration:

1. Configuring and hardening operating systems to minimize vulnerabilities.
2. Implementing security policies, access controls, and encryption.

System Administration:

1. Performing routine system maintenance and updates.
2. Managing user accounts, permissions, and system resources.

Incident Response:

1. Responding to security incidents and conducting forensic analysis.
2. Identifying and mitigating security threats within the operating system.

Patch Management:

1. Implementing effective patch management practices.
2. Ensuring that operating systems are up-to-date with the latest security patches.

Logging and Monitoring:

1. Configuring and analysing system logs for security events.
2. Implementing monitoring solutions to detect and respond to security incidents.

Crafting Your Operating System Proficiency Learning Path

1. Foundational Knowledge:

Begin by building a strong foundation in the fundamentals of operating systems. Understand the architecture, file systems, and basic functionalities of popular operating systems such as Windows, Linux, and macOS. Books like "Operating System Concepts" by Abraham Silberschatz provide a comprehensive introduction.

2. Hands-On Practice:

Gain hands-on experience by setting up virtual machines or installing operating systems on physical hardware. Experiment with different configurations, user permissions, and system settings. Practical experience enhances your understanding of system behavior and administration.

3. Operating System-Specific Courses:

Enroll in courses that focus on specific operating systems commonly used in enterprise environments. Platforms like Udemy, Coursera, and edX offer courses tailored to Windows Server, Linux Administration, and macOS management. Look for courses that include practical labs and real-world scenarios.

4. Certifications in Operating Systems:

1. Obtain certifications that validate your proficiency in specific operating systems. Key certifications include:
2. Microsoft Certified: Windows Server or Windows 10 certifications: Focus on Windows operating systems.

3. CompTIA Linux+ or Red Hat Certified System Administrator (RHCSA): Validate Linux administration skills.
4. Apple Certified Support Professional (ACSP): Demonstrates proficiency in macOS.

5. Security Configuration Practices:

Dive into security configuration practices for operating systems. Learn how to secure user accounts, configure firewalls, enable encryption, and apply security policies. Familiarize yourself with tools and utilities for assessing and enhancing system security.

6. Incident Response Training:

Equip yourself with skills in incident response within operating systems. Understand the common signs of security incidents, conduct forensic analysis, and develop response plans. Training in tools like EnCase, Wireshark, and Sysinternals can be valuable.

7. Logging and Monitoring Tools:

Explore logging and monitoring tools specific to operating systems. Learn how to configure and analyze logs using tools like Windows Event Viewer, syslog, and auditd on Linux. Implement solutions for real-time monitoring of system activities.

Ethical Considerations in Operating System Proficiency

Given the critical role of operating systems in cybersecurity, ethical considerations are paramount. Operating system professionals often deal with sensitive information and have the responsibility to maintain ethical standards. Key ethical considerations include:

Responsible System Administration:

1. Administer systems responsibly, adhering to security best practices and organizational policies.
2. Avoid actions that could compromise the integrity or availability of systems.

Transparent Communication:

1. Clearly communicate system changes, updates, or maintenance activities to stakeholders.
2. Provide advance notice for planned system downtime or changes that may impact users.

Data Privacy and Protection:

1. Uphold data privacy and protection principles when handling sensitive information within operating systems.
2. Implement encryption and access controls to safeguard confidential data.

Responsible Patch Management:

1. Implement timely patch management practices to address security vulnerabilities.
2. Avoid delaying critical security updates that could expose systems to known threats.

Advancing Your Operating System Proficiency

As you progress in your operating system proficiency, consider the following strategies for professional advancement:

Specialization in Specific Operating Systems:

1. Focus on becoming an expert in a specific operating system, such as Windows, Linux, or macOS.
2. Specialization allows for in-depth knowledge and expertise.

Advanced Certifications:

Pursue advanced certifications that demonstrate mastery in operating system security and administration. Examples include the Microsoft Certified: Azure Solutions Architect Expert or Certified Information Systems Security Professional (CISSP).

Integration with Cloud Environments:

1. Gain expertise in integrating operating systems with cloud environments.
2. Understand security considerations and best practices for operating systems in cloud platforms like AWS, Azure, or Google Cloud.

Security Automation:

1. Explore security automation tools and practices for operating systems.
2. Automate routine security configurations and monitoring tasks to enhance efficiency.

Leadership Roles:

1. Aim for leadership roles within IT departments, such as Chief Information Officer (CIO) or Director of IT Operations.
2. Leadership positions involve strategic planning, policy development, and overseeing the execution of operating system initiatives.

Conclusion

Operating system proficiency is a foundational pillar in cybersecurity, providing the expertise needed to secure and manage the digital infrastructure. By crafting a learning path that encompasses foundational knowledge, hands-on experience, and ethical considerations, you can position yourself as a skilled professional capable of navigating the diverse landscapes of operating systems. Embrace the challenges, stay curious, and contribute to the robust security and functionality of digital environments.

Linux and Unix Basics

In the realm of cybersecurity, a profound understanding of operating systems extends to the diverse landscape of Linux and Unix. This chapter explores the critical importance of Linux and Unix Basics in the broader context of Operating System Proficiency. Aspiring cybersecurity professionals will gain insights into the skills, strategies, and learning paths necessary to navigate the complexities of these powerful operating systems.

Understanding Linux and Unix Basics

Overview:

Linux and Unix operating systems form the backbone of many servers, embedded systems, and critical infrastructure components. Proficiency in Linux and Unix is vital for cybersecurity professionals as these systems are prevalent in enterprise environments, cloud services, and networking devices.

Key Skills:

Command-Line Proficiency:

1. Mastery of command-line interfaces (CLI) in Linux and Unix.
2. Efficient navigation, file manipulation, and command execution.

User and Permission Management:

1. Managing user accounts and permissions in a multi-user environment.
2. Understanding the role of sudo and **su** commands.

File System Structure:

1. Familiarity with the hierarchical file system structure.
2. Understanding key directories and their purposes.

Process Management:

1. Monitoring and managing processes on Linux and Unix.
2. Utilizing commands like ps, top, and kill.

Shell Scripting:

1. Writing and executing basic shell scripts.
2. Automating routine tasks using shell scripting.

Crafting Your Linux and Unix Basics Learning Path

1. Familiarity with Command-Line Interfaces:

Start your journey by becoming comfortable with the command-line interfaces of Linux and Unix. Practice navigating directories, listing files, and executing basic commands. Familiarity with the CLI is fundamental for efficient system administration and troubleshooting.

2. Online Courses on Linux Fundamentals:

Enrol in online courses that cover the fundamentals of Linux. Platforms like Linux Academy, Udemy, and edX offer courses tailored to different skill levels. Look for courses that include hands-on labs to reinforce command-line skills and system administration tasks.

3. Linux Certification Programs:

Consider pursuing certifications that validate your proficiency in Linux. The Linux Professional Institute Certification (LPIC) and Red Hat Certified Engineer (RHCE) are well-recognized certifications that cover various aspects of Linux system administration. These certifications often include hands-on exams to assess practical skills.

4. Virtualization and Lab Exercises:

Set up virtual machines or a dedicated lab environment to practice Linux and Unix concepts. Experiment with user and permission management, file system navigation, and basic shell scripting. Virtualization tools like VirtualBox or VMware provide a safe environment for experimentation.

5. Shell Scripting Practice:

Delve into shell scripting to automate repetitive tasks and enhance your efficiency as a Linux and Unix administrator. Learn scripting languages like Bash and Python. Start with simple scripts and gradually progress to more complex automation scenarios.

6. Community Involvement and Forums:

Engage with the Linux and Unix community through forums, social media groups, and conferences. Platforms like Stack Overflow, Reddit (e.g., r/linux), and Linux user groups provide opportunities to seek advice, share knowledge, and stay informed about the latest developments.

Ethical Considerations in Linux and Unix Basics

Given the role of Linux and Unix in critical infrastructure, ethical considerations are paramount. Operating responsibly and ethically in these environments is crucial for maintaining the security and integrity of systems. Key ethical considerations include:

Responsible User and Permission Management:

1. Adhere to the principle of least privilege when managing user accounts and permissions.
2. Avoid granting unnecessary privileges to users, minimizing the risk of unauthorized actions.

Transparent Communication in Shell Scripting:

1. Clearly document shell scripts, especially those that automate critical tasks.
2. Provide comments within scripts to explain functionality, ensuring transparency for other administrators.

Secure Configuration Practices:

1. Implement secure configurations for Linux and Unix systems.
2. Regularly review and update security settings to address evolving threats.

Ethical Use of Open Source Tools:

1. When using open-source tools, adhere to licensing agreements and give proper attribution.
2. Avoid unauthorized modification or distribution of open-source software.

Advancing Your Linux and Unix Proficiency

As you progress in your Linux and Unix proficiency, consider the following strategies for professional advancement:

Advanced Linux Certifications:

Pursue advanced certifications that focus on specific aspects of Linux administration. The Linux Professional Institute offers higher-level certifications, such as LPIC-2 and LPIC-3, allowing you to specialize in areas like network security or enterprise administration.

Specialization in Unix Variants:

1. Explore Unix variants such as AIX, HP-UX, or Solaris, depending on the specific requirements of your organization.
2. Certifications specific to these variants, such as IBM Certified System Administrator - AIX, can enhance your expertise.

Integration with Cloud Environments:

1. Gain expertise in deploying and managing Linux-based systems in cloud environments.
2. Platforms like AWS, Azure, and Google Cloud offer certifications that include Linux-focused content.

Contributions to Open-Source Projects:

1. Contribute to open-source projects related to Linux and Unix.
2. Active participation in the open-source community enhances your visibility and allows you to collaborate with other professionals.

Security Hardening and Monitoring:

1. Specialize in securing Linux and Unix systems by mastering security hardening practices.
2. Develop skills in configuring and monitoring security tools to detect and respond to potential threats.

Conclusion

Linux and Unix proficiency is a cornerstone of cybersecurity, especially in environments where these operating systems are prevalent. By crafting a learning path that encompasses fundamental knowledge, hands-on experience, and ethical considerations, you position yourself as a skilled professional capable of navigating the complexities of Linux and Unix environments. Embrace the challenges, stay engaged with the community, and contribute to the secure and efficient operation of critical systems.

Windows Server and Client Environments

In the intricate tapestry of cybersecurity, mastering Windows Server and Client Environments is like wielding a powerful tool to secure the backbone of many enterprise systems. This chapter explores the indispensable nature of Windows Server and Client Environments in the broader context of Operating System Proficiency. Aspiring cybersecurity professionals will gain insights into the skills, strategies, and learning paths essential to navigate the complexities of these widely used operating systems.

Understanding Windows Server and Client Environments

Overview:

Windows operating systems dominate the corporate landscape, with Windows Server and Client Environments serving as the linchpin for countless organizations. Proficiency in these systems is paramount for cybersecurity professionals, empowering them to secure, configure, and analyse the security posture of both servers and individual workstations.

Key Skills:

Active Directory Management:

1. Mastery of Active Directory (AD) for user and group management.
2. Understanding Group Policies and their role in security configurations.

Server Administration:

1. Efficient administration of Windows Server environments.
2. Configuring and managing services, roles, and features.

Security Configuration in Windows Environments:

1. Implementing security best practices for Windows servers and clients.
2. Utilizing Windows Defender and other security tools.

PowerShell Scripting:

1. Proficiency in PowerShell scripting for automation.
2. Creating scripts for system administration and security tasks.

Client Endpoint Security:

1. Configuring and managing security settings on Windows client machines.
2. Deploying and managing antivirus and anti-malware solutions.

Crafting Your Windows Server and Client Environments Learning Path

1. Active Directory Mastery: Begin your journey by acquiring a deep understanding of Active Directory. Learn to create and manage user accounts, groups, and organizational units. Explore the intricacies of Group Policy to enforce security settings across a Windows environment.

2. Online Courses on Windows Server Administration:

Enroll in online courses that focus on Windows Server administration. Platforms like Microsoft Learn, Udemy, and Pluralsight offer courses covering a range of skill levels. Look for courses that include hands-on labs to reinforce server administration tasks.

3. Windows Server Certifications:

Consider pursuing certifications that validate your proficiency in Windows Server environments. The Microsoft Certified: Azure Administrator Associate and Microsoft Certified: Windows Server certifications are valuable credentials that cover server administration and security. Certification exams often include practical scenarios to assess real-world skills.

4. Security Configuration in Windows Environments:

Delve into security configurations specific to Windows Server and Client Environments. Learn how to harden servers, implement secure authentication mechanisms, and configure firewall settings. Familiarize yourself with Windows Defender and other security tools for threat detection and mitigation.

5. PowerShell Scripting Practice:

Develop proficiency in PowerShell scripting for Windows environments. Create scripts to automate routine administrative tasks, security configurations, and system monitoring. PowerShell's versatility makes it a powerful tool for managing Windows systems efficiently.

6. Endpoint Security Practices:

Explore endpoint security practices for Windows client machines. Understand the nuances of configuring Windows Defender and other security features. Learn to deploy and manage antivirus solutions to protect client endpoints from malware and other threats.

7. Hands-On Labs and Simulations:

Set up labs or use simulation tools to gain hands-on experience with Windows Server and Client Environments. Tools like Hyper-V or VirtualBox allow you to create virtual environments for testing configurations and scenarios without impacting production systems.

Ethical Considerations in Windows Server and Client Environments

Given the prevalence of Windows environments in enterprise settings, ethical considerations are crucial. Operating ethically in Windows Server and Client Environments is essential for maintaining the security and trust of organizational systems. Key ethical considerations include:

Responsible Active Directory Management:

1. Administer Active Directory responsibly, adhering to the principle of least privilege.
2. Avoid actions that could disrupt user access or compromise sensitive information.

Transparent Communication in Scripting:

1. Clearly document PowerShell scripts, especially those that impact security configurations.
2. Provide documentation on script functionality and intended outcomes.

Secure Configuration Practices:

1. Implement secure configurations for Windows servers and clients.
2. Regularly review and update security settings to address emerging threats.

Ethical Use of Security Tools:

1. Use security tools and features within Windows environments ethically and responsibly.
2. Avoid unauthorized access or manipulation of security settings for malicious purposes.

Advancing Your Windows Server and Client Environments Proficiency

As you progress in your proficiency with Windows Server and Client Environments, consider the following strategies for professional advancement:

Advanced Windows Certifications:

Pursue advanced certifications that focus on specific aspects of Windows Server administration and security. The Microsoft Certified: Azure Solutions Architect Expert and Microsoft Certified: Enterprise Administrator Expert are examples of advanced certifications that demonstrate mastery.

Integration with Cloud Environments:

1. Gain expertise in integrating Windows environments with cloud platforms such as Azure.
2. Certifications like Microsoft Certified: Azure Administrator Associate cover cloud integration and administration.

Security Monitoring and Incident Response:

1. Specialize in security monitoring and incident response within Windows environments.

2. Develop skills in using Windows Event Viewer, Microsoft Defender ATP, and other tools for detecting and responding to security incidents.

Contributions to Windows Community:

1. Contribute to the Windows community through forums, blogs, or open-source projects.
2. Actively engage with other professionals to share knowledge and insights.

Leadership Roles in IT Security:

1. Aim for leadership roles within IT security teams or departments.
2. Leadership positions involve strategic planning, policy development, and overseeing security initiatives.

Conclusion

Proficiency in Windows Server and Client Environments is a fundamental aspect of cybersecurity, given the widespread use of Windows systems in organizational settings. By crafting a learning path that encompasses foundational knowledge, hands-on experience, and ethical considerations, you position yourself as a skilled professional capable of securing and optimizing Windows environments. Embrace the challenges, stay informed about evolving technologies, and contribute to the robust security and functionality of Windows-based systems.

Coding and Scripting Skills

In the intricate world of cybersecurity, possessing robust coding and scripting skills is akin to wielding a powerful toolset. This chapter delves into the pivotal role that coding and scripting skills play in laying a solid foundation for a successful career in cybersecurity. As an experienced professional, I will guide you through the significance of these skills, their practical applications, and a strategic approach to mastering them.

Why Coding and Scripting Skills Are Crucial in Cybersecurity

1. Automating Security Operations:

Coding and scripting empower cybersecurity professionals to automate routine and time-consuming tasks. This is particularly crucial in security operations where rapid response is essential. Automation allows for the swift analysis of security logs, routine vulnerability assessments, and the deployment of security patches, freeing up valuable time for more complex tasks.

2. Threat Analysis and Intelligence:

Understanding and countering evolving cyber threats require a deep dive into their mechanics. Coding skills enable professionals to develop tools for threat analysis, allowing for the identification of patterns, anomalies, and potential vulnerabilities. Scripting languages such as Python or PowerShell are commonly used to parse and analyze large datasets to extract actionable intelligence.

3. Customization of Security Solutions:

Off-the-shelf security solutions may not always align perfectly with the unique needs of an organization. Coding skills empower cybersecurity professionals to tailor existing tools or build custom solutions. This flexibility ensures that the security infrastructure is finely tuned to the organization's specific requirements, enhancing overall efficacy.

4. Incident Response and Forensics:

In the aftermath of a security incident, the ability to rapidly respond and conduct forensic analysis is paramount. Coding skills allow professionals to develop scripts and tools that facilitate swift incident response, aiding in the containment of threats and the subsequent forensic investigation to understand the extent of the breach.

5. Developing and Analysing Malware:

Combatting malware requires an in-depth understanding of its code. Coding skills enable cybersecurity professionals to dissect and analyse malicious code, helping in the development of effective countermeasures. This skill is crucial in a proactive approach to cybersecurity, where anticipating and neutralizing potential threats is a constant endeavour.

Crafting Your Learning Path: A Strategic Approach

1. Selecting the Right Programming Language:

The first step in your journey to mastering coding and scripting is selecting the right programming language. Python is widely regarded as an excellent starting point due to its readability, versatility, and extensive libraries. PowerShell and Bash are also highly valuable for scripting, especially in Windows and Unix environments, respectively.

2. Engaging in Online Courses and Tutorials:

Numerous online platforms offer courses tailored to cybersecurity professionals. Platforms such as Codecademy, Coursera, and Udemy provide comprehensive courses on Python, scripting, and automation. These courses often cater specifically to the cybersecurity domain, ensuring relevance to your career goals.

3. Participating in Capture The Flag (CTF) Challenges:

Engaging in CTF challenges provides a practical and gamified approach to learning coding skills. CTFs often involve writing scripts to solve challenges, simulating real-world scenarios. Platforms like Hack The Box and OverTheWire offer a variety of challenges suitable for different skill levels.

4. Building Personal Projects:

The best way to solidify coding skills is through hands-on experience. Develop small projects that align with your cybersecurity interests. This could include creating automated security scans, log analysers, or scripts for network monitoring. These projects serve as tangible evidence of your skills and contribute to your professional portfolio.

5. Collaborating with the Cybersecurity Community:

Joining online forums, community platforms, and social media groups dedicated to cybersecurity allows you to learn from others, share knowledge, and collaborate on coding projects. The cybersecurity community is known for its openness and willingness to help newcomers, making it an invaluable resource for your learning journey.

6. Continuous Learning and Specialization:

Coding proficiency is not a static skill but a dynamic one that requires continuous learning. Stay informed about updates in coding languages, emerging technologies, and new tools relevant to cybersecurity. Consider specializing in areas such as penetration testing, malware analysis, or automation to further enhance your expertise.

Overcoming Challenges and Maximizing Learning

1. Patience and Persistence:

Learning to code is a journey that requires patience and persistence. Understand that challenges are a natural part of the process, and each obstacle is an opportunity to learn and grow. Celebrate your successes, no matter how small, and keep pushing forward.

2. Apply Coding to Real-World Scenarios:

To maximize your learning, always strive to apply coding skills to real-world cybersecurity scenarios. Whether it's scripting for a penetration test or automating security response procedures, practical application reinforces theoretical knowledge and prepares you for the challenges you'll face in your professional role.

3. Seek Feedback and Mentorship:

Actively seek feedback on your code from peers or mentors. Learning from others' experiences and benefiting from constructive criticism accelerates your learning curve. Mentorship can provide valuable insights, guidance, and shortcuts to help you navigate the complexities of coding in a cybersecurity context.

4. Stay Informed About Industry Trends:

The field of cybersecurity is dynamic, and coding practices evolve. Regularly read industry blogs, attend conferences, and participate in webinars to stay informed about the latest trends, tools, and best practices. Being aware of industry developments ensures that your coding skills remain relevant and effective.

Conclusion: Building a Foundation for Cybersecurity Excellence

In conclusion, coding and scripting skills are foundational to a successful career in cybersecurity. They empower professionals to navigate the intricacies of cyber threats, automate routine tasks, and contribute significantly to the security posture of organizations. By strategically approaching the learning process, engaging with the cybersecurity community, and continuously refining your skills, you are not only building a solid foundation but also positioning yourself for success in the dynamic and ever-evolving field of cybersecurity.

Python for Security Professionals

In the realm of cybersecurity, the ability to code is a fundamental skill that sets apart effective professionals from the rest. Among the myriad of programming languages available, Python stands out as a versatile and powerful tool for security professionals. This section explores why Python is a preferred language, its applications in cybersecurity, and a strategic approach to mastering it.

Why Python for Security Professionals?

1. Readability and Versatility:

Python is celebrated for its readability, making it an ideal language for both beginners and experienced developers. Its syntax is clear and concise, enabling security professionals to write efficient and understandable code. Additionally, Python's versatility allows it to be applied across various domains within cybersecurity.

2. Extensive Libraries and Frameworks:

Python boasts a rich ecosystem of libraries and frameworks that significantly expedite development. For security professionals, this means access to powerful tools and modules for tasks such as network analysis, penetration testing, and data manipulation. Notable libraries like Scapy, Requests, and BeautifulSoup are indispensable in cybersecurity projects.

3. Community Support:

Python's community is vibrant and supportive, providing an invaluable resource for security professionals. Online forums, documentation, and collaborative platforms like GitHub offer a wealth of knowledge and shared projects. Leveraging this community support accelerates the learning process and aids in troubleshooting challenges.

73

4. Platform Independence:

Python's platform independence allows security professionals to write code that runs seamlessly across different operating systems. This flexibility is crucial in cybersecurity, where practitioners often work in heterogeneous environments. Whether analyzing logs on a Linux server or scripting in a Windows environment, Python ensures consistency.

5. Integration with Other Tools:

Python's ability to integrate with other languages and tools enhances its utility in cybersecurity. Security professionals can seamlessly incorporate Python scripts into existing workflows, enhancing automation and orchestration capabilities. This interoperability is essential for creating holistic cybersecurity solutions.

Mastering Python for Cybersecurity: A Strategic Approach

1. Foundations of Python:

Start your Python journey by grasping the basics. Familiarize yourself with variables, data types, loops, and conditional statements. Numerous online platforms, including Codecademy and Real Python, offer interactive courses that cater specifically to cybersecurity professionals.

2. Cybersecurity-Specific Python Libraries:

Explore Python libraries tailored for cybersecurity. Begin with libraries like Requests for HTTP requests, Scapy for packet manipulation, and Paramiko for SSH protocol implementation. Understanding these libraries equips you with essential tools for tasks ranging from network reconnaissance to secure communication.

3. Hands-On Projects:

The most effective way to solidify your Python skills is through hands-on projects. Consider creating a network scanner, a simple intrusion detection system, or an automated vulnerability scanner. These projects not only enhance your coding proficiency but also serve as practical applications of cybersecurity concepts.

4. Capture The Flag (CTF) Challenges:

Engage in CTF challenges that specifically require Python scripting. Platforms like Hack The Box frequently feature challenges where Python skills are essential for solving puzzles, exploiting vulnerabilities, or automating tasks. CTFs provide a gamified environment to hone your skills in real-world scenarios.

5. Advanced Topics:

Progress to advanced Python topics relevant to cybersecurity. Explore topics such as multithreading and multiprocessing for parallel processing, cryptography for secure communication, and web scraping for data gathering. Mastery of these advanced topics expands your toolkit and prepares you for complex cybersecurity tasks.

6. Build a Portfolio:

Assemble a portfolio showcasing your Python projects and their applications in cybersecurity. This portfolio serves as a tangible representation of your skills and accomplishments. Potential employers and collaborators can review your portfolio to gauge your proficiency and practical experience.

Challenges and Solutions in Learning Python

1. Overcoming Learning Plateaus:

Learning Python, like any skill, may encounter plateaus where progress seems slow. Patience and persistence are crucial during these phases. Seek out new challenges, explore different aspects of Python, and consider collaborating on open-source projects to reignite your passion for learning.

2. Real-World Application:

Ensure that your learning is grounded in real-world application. Whenever you learn a new Python concept, immediately apply it to a cybersecurity scenario. This practical approach reinforces theoretical knowledge and accelerates your ability to tackle challenges encountered in professional settings.

3. Staying Updated:

Python is a dynamic language with frequent updates and new releases. Stay informed about the latest features, libraries, and best practices. Subscribe to Python-related newsletters, follow key influencers on social media, and participate in Python communities to stay ahead of emerging trends.

4. Collaboration and Feedback:

Seek collaboration with peers and mentors within the cybersecurity and Python communities. Share your Python projects, seek feedback, and learn from others' experiences. Constructive criticism accelerates your learning curve and exposes you to different approaches and perspectives.

Conclusion: Python as Your Cybersecurity Ally

In conclusion, mastering Python is a strategic move for any aspiring or seasoned cybersecurity professional. Its readability, versatility, and vast ecosystem of libraries make it an indispensable tool in the security practitioner's arsenal. By strategically approaching Python learning, engaging with the cybersecurity community, and continuously challenging yourself with hands-on projects, you are not only building a solid foundation but also positioning yourself for success in the dynamic field of cybersecurity. Python isn't just a programming language; it's your ally in navigating the complexities of cybersecurity with precision and efficiency.

Scripting for Automation

In the dynamic field of cybersecurity, automation is the linchpin that accelerates and fortifies defense strategies. Scripting for automation is a core skill that empowers cybersecurity professionals to streamline workflows, enhance incident response, and proactively address security challenges. In this section, we will delve into the significance of scripting for automation, its practical applications, and a strategic approach to mastering this crucial skill.

The Power of Scripting for Automation in Cybersecurity

1. Efficiency and Time Savings:

Scripting enables the automation of repetitive and time-consuming tasks, freeing up valuable time for cybersecurity professionals. Whether it's conducting routine vulnerability scans, parsing log files, or deploying security updates, automation through scripting ensures that these tasks are executed swiftly and consistently.

2. Rapid Incident Response:

In the face of a security incident, time is of the essence. Scripting allows for the rapid development of automated incident response procedures. From isolating compromised systems to collecting forensic data, automation through scripts ensures a swift and coordinated response, minimizing the impact of security breaches.

3. Consistency and Accuracy:

Manual execution of tasks introduces the risk of human error. Scripting ensures consistency and accuracy in the execution of security processes. Automated scripts follow predefined procedures, reducing the likelihood of mistakes and ensuring that security measures are applied uniformly across systems.

4. Scalability and Adaptability:

As organizations grow and cybersecurity challenges evolve, the ability to scale security operations becomes paramount. Scripting allows professionals to create scalable and adaptable solutions. Whether it's scaling up the deployment of security patches or adjusting incident response procedures, scripted automation ensures flexibility and agility.

5. Customization for Specific Environments:

Security environments vary, and off-the-shelf solutions may not always align with the unique requirements of an organization. Scripting provides the flexibility to customize security processes for specific environments. Cybersecurity professionals can tailor scripts to the nuances of their infrastructure, ensuring a bespoke and effective security posture.

Strategic Approach to Scripting for Automation

1. Identifying Automation Opportunities:

Begin by identifying tasks within your cybersecurity workflow that can benefit from automation. These could include tasks such as log analysis, vulnerability assessments, or routine system checks. Prioritize tasks that are repetitive, time-consuming, and can be codified into a script.

2. Selecting the Right Scripting Language:

Choose a scripting language that aligns with the specific automation task at hand. Python, PowerShell, and Bash are popular choices in the cybersecurity domain. Python, with its readability and extensive libraries, is often preferred for its versatility, while PowerShell is advantageous in Windows-centric environments, and Bash is widely used in Unix/Linux environments.

3. Learning Scripting Language Basics:

Familiarize yourself with the basics of the selected scripting language. Understand variables, loops, conditional statements, and functions. Online platforms like Codecademy, Udemy, and others offer courses specifically tailored for cybersecurity professionals, providing a structured learning path for scripting.

4. Hands-On Automation Projects:

The most effective way to learn scripting for automation is through hands-on projects. Start with small, manageable projects and gradually progress to more complex tasks. For example, automate the retrieval and analysis of log files, create a script for routine system checks, or develop a script to automate security policy enforcement.

5. Utilizing Built-In Functions and Libraries:

Leverage the built-in functions and libraries of your chosen scripting language. Python's rich ecosystem of libraries, PowerShell's integration with Windows systems, and Bash's powerful command-line capabilities provide a wealth of resources. This not only expedites script development but also ensures that your scripts are efficient and robust.

6. Version Control and Documentation:

Implement version control for your scripts using platforms like Git. This ensures that you can track changes, collaborate with others, and roll back to previous versions if needed. Additionally, maintain thorough documentation for your scripts, including comments within the code, to enhance readability and facilitate knowledge transfer.

Challenges and Solutions in Scripting for Automation

1. Overcoming Resistance to Change:

Introducing automation may face resistance from those accustomed to manual processes. Communicate the benefits of automation, showcase time savings, and emphasize the potential for improved security through consistent and accurate execution of tasks.

2. Addressing Security Concerns:

Security professionals must be mindful of the security implications of automation. Ensure that scripts adhere to security best practices, encrypt sensitive information, and undergo rigorous testing. Regularly review and update scripts to address emerging threats and vulnerabilities.

3. Scaling Automation Solutions:

As organizations grow, the scalability of automation solutions becomes crucial. Design scripts with scalability in mind, using modular and reusable code. Consider the potential expansion of the environment and ensure that scripts can adapt to changing requirements.

4. Balancing Automation and Human Oversight:

While automation is powerful, it should complement, not replace, human oversight. Ensure that critical security processes involve human review and intervention where necessary. Automation should enhance human capabilities rather than entirely supplant them.

Conclusion: Mastering Scripting for Cybersecurity Excellence

In conclusion, scripting for automation is a cornerstone skill for cybersecurity professionals. It empowers practitioners to enhance efficiency, respond rapidly to incidents, and maintain a consistent and accurate security posture. By strategically approaching scripting, identifying automation opportunities, selecting the right scripting language, and leveraging built-in functions and libraries, you are not just coding; you are orchestrating a resilient and dynamic cybersecurity strategy. Embrace the challenges, continuously refine your scripts, and position yourself as a cybersecurity professional who not only understands the importance of automation but also masters the art of scripting for excellence.

Chapter 5: Mastering Cybersecurity Tools

Introduction to Cybersecurity Tools

In the ever-evolving landscape of cybersecurity, the effectiveness of security professionals often hinges on their proficiency with a diverse array of tools. This chapter serves as a foundational guide, introducing the essential cybersecurity tools that are instrumental in safeguarding digital assets, detecting threats, and responding to incidents. As an experienced cybersecurity professional, I will navigate through the critical components of a security toolkit, shedding light on their applications and strategic use in securing digital environments.

The Role of Cybersecurity Tools

Cybersecurity tools are instrumental in fortifying the digital perimeter, identifying vulnerabilities, and responding to potential threats. These tools are designed to streamline complex processes, automate routine tasks, and provide real-time insights into the security posture of an organization. Whether you are a novice entering the field or a seasoned professional seeking to broaden your toolkit, understanding the fundamental categories of cybersecurity tools is essential.

Categories of Cybersecurity Tools

1. Vulnerability Scanning Tools:

Vulnerability scanners play a pivotal role in identifying weaknesses within a system or network. Tools such as Nessus, OpenVAS, and Qualys scan for known vulnerabilities, misconfigurations, and potential entry points that malicious actors could exploit. These tools provide a foundational assessment of an organization's security posture, allowing for timely remediation.

2. Network Security Tools:

Network security tools are designed to protect the integrity and confidentiality of data traversing a network. Firewalls, intrusion detection/prevention systems (IDS/IPS), and virtual private networks (VPNs) are examples of network security tools. These tools serves as the first line of defense, monitoring and filtering incoming and outgoing network traffic to prevent unauthorized access.

3. Endpoint Security Tools:

Endpoints, including computers, servers, and mobile devices, are common targets for cyber threats. Endpoint security tools, such as antivirus software, endpoint detection and response (EDR) solutions, and host-based firewalls, are crucial for detecting and mitigating threats at the device level. These tools protect against malware, ransomware, and other malicious activities.

4. Security Information and Event Management (SIEM) Tools:

SIEM tools aggregate and analyze log data from various sources within an organization's IT infrastructure. Platforms like Splunk, ELK Stack, and IBM QRadar provide real-time insights into security events, enabling security professionals to detect anomalies, investigate incidents, and respond proactively to potential threats.

5. Incident Response Tools:

Incident response tools facilitate the coordination and management of cybersecurity incidents. Platforms like CyberArk, Carbon Black, and IBM Resilient assist in identifying, containing, eradicating, recovering from, and learning from security incidents. These tools are crucial for minimizing the impact of a breach and ensuring a swift and organized response.

6. Encryption Tools:

Encryption tools are vital for securing sensitive data both in transit and at rest. Secure Sockets Layer (SSL) and Transport Layer Security (TLS) protocols encrypt communication over the internet, while tools like VeraCrypt and BitLocker provide encryption for data storage. These tools ensure the confidentiality and integrity of sensitive information.

7. Penetration Testing Tools:

Penetration testing tools simulate cyber attacks to identify vulnerabilities in a system or network. Tools such as Metasploit, Burp Suite, and Wireshark are commonly used by ethical hackers and security professionals to assess the security robustness of an organization's infrastructure. These tools help uncover potential weaknesses before malicious actors can exploit them.

8. Forensic Analysis Tools:

Forensic analysis tools aid in the investigation of security incidents and gathering evidence for legal purposes. Tools like EnCase, Autopsy, and FTK (Forensic Toolkit) assist cybersecurity professionals in examining digital artifacts, recovering deleted files, and reconstructing the sequence of events during a security incident.

Strategic Use of Cybersecurity Tools

1. Comprehensive Security Strategy:

A successful cybersecurity strategy requires a holistic approach that leverages a variety of tools. Instead of relying solely on one category of tools, organizations should adopt a comprehensive security strategy that integrates vulnerability management, network security, endpoint protection, and incident response.

2. Continuous Monitoring and Threat Detection:

Cyber threats are constantly evolving, necessitating continuous monitoring and detection. SIEM tools play a crucial role in aggregating and analyzing logs from various sources, enabling security professionals to detect and respond to security incidents in real time. Continuous monitoring ensures that security teams stay ahead of emerging threats.

3. Automation for Efficiency:

Automation is a force multiplier in cybersecurity. Tools that automate routine tasks, such as vulnerability scanning and incident response, enable security professionals to focus on more complex and strategic aspects of their roles. By automating repetitive processes, organizations can respond swiftly to threats and ensure consistent security measures.

4. Integration of Tools for Synergy:

The effectiveness of cybersecurity tools is amplified when they work seamlessly together. Integration between tools allows for a synergistic approach to security. For example, integrating vulnerability scanning results into the SIEM platform enhances the correlation of events, providing a more comprehensive view of the security landscape.

5. Regular Training and Skill Development:

Cybersecurity tools are most effective in the hands of skilled professionals. Regular training and skill development programs ensure that security teams are proficient in the use of tools and stay abreast of the latest features and updates. This continuous learning approach is essential in a field where technology evolves rapidly.

Challenges and Solutions in Implementing Cybersecurity Tools

1. Tool Overload and Integration Challenges:

The multitude of cybersecurity tools available can lead to tool overload, where organizations struggle to manage and integrate diverse solutions.

To address this, conduct a thorough assessment of the organization's needs, prioritize tools based on their relevance, and focus on seamless integration for improved effectiveness.

2. Resource Constraints:

Small and medium-sized enterprises (SMEs) may face resource constraints when implementing cybersecurity tools. Cloud-based security solutions and managed security service providers (MSSPs) offer cost-effective alternatives. Additionally, organizations can prioritize foundational tools based on their immediate security needs.

3. Human Error and Training Gaps:

Human error, often resulting from a lack of training, can hinder the effective use of cybersecurity tools. Establish comprehensive training programs to ensure that security professionals are proficient in tool usage. Implementing user-friendly interfaces and providing detailed documentation can also mitigate training gaps.

Conclusion: Navigating the Cybersecurity Tool Landscape

In conclusion, cybersecurity tools are indispensable assets in the defense against evolving cyber threats. From vulnerability management to incident response, each category of tools plays a unique role in fortifying digital environments. Aspiring cybersecurity professionals and seasoned experts alike must understand the diverse tool landscape, strategically integrate these tools into their security arsenal, and continuously adapt to emerging challenges. The journey to mastering cybersecurity tools is not only about technical proficiency but also about adopting a strategic mindset that aligns tools with organizational goals and ensures a resilient defense against cyber adversaries.

Wireshark for Network Analysis

In the vast and intricate landscape of cybersecurity, mastery of tools is paramount. As we delve into the arsenal of cybersecurity tools, we encounter a diverse range designed to address specific challenges in securing digital environments. Among these, Wireshark stands out as a versatile and powerful tool for network analysis. In this section, we will explore the significance of Wireshark, its practical applications, and how mastering this tool can elevate your capabilities in network security.

Understanding the Role of Wireshark in Cybersecurity

1. Network Analysis and Packet Sniffing:

Wireshark, a popular open-source network protocol analyzer, plays a pivotal role in network security by allowing professionals to capture and analyze packets traversing a network. This process, known as packet sniffing, provides invaluable insights into network traffic, enabling cybersecurity experts to identify anomalies, detect suspicious activities, and troubleshoot network issues.

2. Versatility in Protocol Analysis:

Wireshark supports a wide array of network protocols, making it a versatile tool for professionals involved in network security, administration, and troubleshooting. Whether dealing with traditional protocols like TCP/IP or exploring newer technologies, Wireshark's capability to dissect and analyze different protocols positions it as an indispensable asset in understanding network communications.

3. Real-Time and Offline Analysis:

Wireshark facilitates both real-time and offline analysis. In real-time mode, it captures and displays packets as they traverse the network, providing instantaneous insights into ongoing activities. In offline mode, analysts can dissect previously captured traffic, allowing for in-depth retrospective analysis and investigation of historical network events.

4. Identifying Network Threats:

By scrutinizing network traffic, Wireshark assists cybersecurity professionals in identifying potential threats such as malicious traffic, suspicious patterns, or unauthorized communications. Understanding the normal baseline of network behavior empowers professionals to spot anomalies indicative of security incidents, allowing for a proactive response to potential threats.

Practical Applications of Wireshark in Cybersecurity

1. Network Troubleshooting:

Wireshark is an invaluable tool for troubleshooting network issues. When confronted with connectivity problems, performance issues, or unexpected network behavior, network administrators and security professionals can use Wireshark to capture and analyze packets, pinpointing the root cause of the problem and facilitating swift resolution.

2. Security Incident Response:

In the event of a security incident, Wireshark becomes a critical tool for incident response. Analysts can use it to analyze captured packets, identify the source and nature of the attack, and gather evidence for further investigation. Wireshark aids in understanding the tactics and techniques employed by adversaries, guiding a comprehensive response strategy.

3. Traffic Analysis and Baseline Establishment:

Wireshark allows cybersecurity professionals to establish a baseline of normal network behavior by analyzing regular traffic patterns. This baseline becomes instrumental in detecting deviations and anomalies that may indicate a security threat. Continuous traffic analysis using Wireshark contributes to a proactive security stance.

4. Vulnerability Identification:

Wireshark aids in the identification of vulnerabilities by revealing potential security weaknesses in network protocols and configurations. Security professionals can use Wireshark to analyze packet payloads, inspect headers, and identify areas where security measures may need reinforcement to prevent exploitation by malicious actors.

Mastering Wireshark: A Strategic Approach

1. Understanding the Wireshark Interface:

Start by familiarizing yourself with the Wireshark interface. Understand the various panels, filters, and menu options. Wireshark's user-friendly interface allows for intuitive navigation and efficient packet analysis. Online tutorials and documentation can provide valuable insights into navigating the tool effectively.

2. Filtering and Display Options:

Wireshark offers powerful filtering capabilities to focus on specific packets of interest. Learn to create filters based on criteria such as source or destination IP addresses, protocols, or specific keywords. Mastering filtering allows you to zero in on relevant information within large packet captures.

3. Protocols and Decoding:

Wireshark's strength lies in its ability to decode a multitude of network protocols. Invest time in understanding how Wireshark decodes different protocols, ranging from common ones like TCP and UDP to more specialized protocols. This knowledge enhances your ability to dissect and interpret packet contents accurately.

4. Capturing and Saving Packets:

Learn the art of capturing packets efficiently. Wireshark provides options for capturing live traffic on different network interfaces. Understand how to save captured packets in various formats for later analysis. This skill is crucial for both real-time analysis and offline investigation.

5. Analyzing Real-World Scenarios:

The best way to master Wireshark is through practical application. Engage in real-world scenarios such as capturing and analyzing traffic during a simulated security incident, troubleshooting network issues, or examining the impact of specific network configurations. Practical experience enhances your proficiency and problem-solving skills.

Challenges and Solutions in Mastering Wireshark

1. Information Overload:

Wireshark captures a vast amount of information, and beginners may feel overwhelmed. To address this challenge, focus on specific aspects of Wireshark at a time. Gradually expand your knowledge by exploring additional features and functionalities, and regularly practice analyzing different types of traffic.

2. Interpreting Packet Contents:

Interpreting packet contents requires understanding various protocols and their structures. To overcome this challenge, invest time in studying common network protocols and their specifications. Wireshark provides extensive documentation and resources that can aid in deciphering packet payloads and headers.

3. Keeping Pace with Updates:

Wireshark is regularly updated to include support for new protocols and features. To stay current, regularly check for updates and explore new functionalities introduced in each release. Online communities and forums are excellent resources for staying informed about the latest developments and best practices.

Conclusion: Wireshark as a Gateway to Network Mastery

In conclusion, mastering Wireshark is synonymous with gaining a profound understanding of network communications. As a versatile and powerful tool, Wireshark empowers cybersecurity professionals to dissect, analyze, and interpret network traffic, leading to enhanced security measures and effective incident response. By strategically approaching Wireshark through practical application, continuous learning, and real-world scenarios, you not only elevate your proficiency in network analysis but also position yourself as a skilled cybersecurity professional capable of navigating the complexities of the digital landscape with precision and insight.

Metasploit for Penetration Testing

In the realm of cybersecurity, where the adversaries are as dynamic as the technology they target, mastering the right tools is crucial. One such tool that stands at the forefront of offensive security is Metasploit. In this section, we will explore the significance of Metasploit, its practical applications, and how understanding and mastering this tool can elevate your skills in penetration testing.

Understanding the Role of Metasploit in Cybersecurity

1. Open-Source Penetration Testing Framework:

Metasploit is not just a tool; it's a comprehensive penetration testing framework that empowers cybersecurity professionals to assess and exploit vulnerabilities in systems and networks. As an open-source project, Metasploit provides a flexible and extensible platform for ethical hacking, allowing security practitioners to simulate real-world attacks in a controlled environment.

2. Exploitation and Post-Exploitation Framework:

At its core, Metasploit facilitates the identification and exploitation of vulnerabilities. It enables security professionals to launch a variety of attacks, from simple to sophisticated, against target systems. Beyond exploitation, Metasploit offers post-exploitation modules that allow practitioners to maintain access, gather intelligence, and simulate the actions of malicious actors after a successful compromise.

3. Modular Architecture:

Metasploit's strength lies in its modular architecture, comprising a vast array of modules for different stages of the penetration testing lifecycle. From reconnaissance to exploitation, post-exploitation, and even evasion, each module serves a specific purpose, offering flexibility and customization for a wide range of scenarios.

4. Community-Driven Development:

Metasploit benefits from a robust and active community of security professionals, researchers, and developers. This community-driven approach ensures that Metasploit stays current with the latest exploits, vulnerabilities, and attack techniques. The collaborative nature of Metasploit's development fosters a dynamic tool that evolves with the ever-changing threat landscape.

Practical Applications of Metasploit in Cybersecurity

1. Vulnerability Assessment and Exploitation:

Metasploit is a go-to tool for conducting vulnerability assessments and exploiting identified weaknesses. By leveraging a vast database of exploits, security professionals can simulate attacks to assess the resilience of systems and networks. Metasploit streamlines the process of identifying and validating vulnerabilities, allowing for targeted and effective penetration testing.

2. Penetration Testing and Red Teaming:

Metasploit is a staple in the toolkit of penetration testers and red teamers. Whether conducting authorized simulated attacks for organizations or emulating sophisticated adversaries in red team engagements, Metasploit provides the necessary tools and capabilities to assess security defenses, identify weaknesses, and help organizations bolster their security posture.

3. Post-Exploitation and Lateral Movement:

Beyond initial exploitation, Metasploit offers post-exploitation modules that enable security professionals to perform various actions on compromised systems. This includes gathering sensitive information, pivoting to other systems within the network, and maintaining persistent access. Understanding post-exploitation techniques is crucial for simulating realistic attack scenarios.

4. Payloads and Evasion Techniques:

Metasploit allows security professionals to generate and deploy payloads—code that performs specific actions on a target system. Payloads can be tailored to deliver a variety of outcomes, from establishing remote access to capturing credentials. Metasploit also provides evasion techniques to bypass security controls, making it a versatile tool for testing an organization's resilience against advanced adversaries.

Mastering Metasploit: A Strategic Approach

1. Familiarizing Yourself with the Metasploit Framework:

Start by familiarizing yourself with the Metasploit framework. Understand its structure, components, and the basic commands for navigating the interface. Metasploit has a steep learning curve, but investing time in getting comfortable with its environment lays a solid foundation for more advanced usage.

2. Exploring Modules and Exploits:

Metasploit's strength lies in its extensive collection of modules and exploits. Explore the different modules available for reconnaissance, scanning, exploitation, and post-exploitation. Understand the parameters and options associated with each module. Hands-on experimentation with various exploits and payloads enhances your proficiency.

3. Hands-On Penetration Testing Projects:

The best way to master Metasploit is through hands-on projects. Set up a lab environment with virtual machines and simulate penetration testing scenarios. Practice identifying vulnerabilities, exploiting systems, and using post-exploitation techniques. Real-world application of Metasploit's capabilities reinforces theoretical knowledge.

4. Understanding Payloads and Encoders:

Payloads and encoders are integral components of Metasploit. Learn about different types of payloads, their functionalities, and how to customize them for specific scenarios. Understand the role of encoders in evading detection and delivering payloads successfully. This knowledge is crucial for tailoring attacks to bypass security controls.

5. Community Engagement and Continuous Learning:

Engage with the Metasploit community to stay updated on the latest developments, exploits, and techniques. Participate in forums, read community-contributed content, and follow key contributors. Metasploit's dynamic nature means that continuous learning is essential to stay abreast of emerging threats and advancements.

Challenges and Solutions in Mastering Metasploit

1. Legal and Ethical Considerations:

Metasploit is a powerful tool that, if misused, can lead to legal and ethical concerns. Ensure that you use Metasploit in ethical and legal scenarios, such as authorized penetration testing engagements or personal learning environments. Understand the importance of obtaining proper authorization before conducting any penetration testing activities.

2. Complexity of the Framework:

Metasploit's extensive capabilities come with a level of complexity. To overcome this, break down your learning into manageable components.

Focus on specific modules, exploits, or techniques, and gradually expand your knowledge. Refer to Metasploit's documentation and online resources to navigate its complexities effectively.

3. Keeping Abreast of Updates:

Metasploit is actively developed, and updates are released regularly. To stay current, subscribe to relevant channels, follow the official Metasploit blog, and engage with the community. Regularly updating your Metasploit installation ensures that you have access to the latest exploits, features, and improvements.

Conclusion: Metasploit as a Catalyst for Cybersecurity Excellence

In conclusion, mastering Metasploit is not just about learning a tool; it's about acquiring a skill set that is instrumental in assessing and enhancing the security posture of organizations. Metasploit empowers cybersecurity professionals to think like adversaries, identify vulnerabilities, and simulate sophisticated attacks. By strategically approaching Metasploit through hands-on projects, continuous learning, and community engagement, you position yourself as a skilled professional capable of navigating the complexities of offensive security. Metasploit is not just a tool in your arsenal; it's a catalyst for excellence in cybersecurity, propelling you to the forefront of the ever-evolving landscape of digital defence.

SIEM (Security Information and Event Management) Tools

In the dynamic landscape of cybersecurity, the effective management of security information and events is paramount. Security Information and Event Management (SIEM) tools play a pivotal role in this domain, providing organizations with the capability to aggregate, analyze, and respond to security events in real-time. In this section, we will explore the significance of SIEM tools, their practical applications, and the strategic approach to mastering these tools for a robust cybersecurity posture.

Understanding the Role of SIEM Tools in Cybersecurity

1. Comprehensive Event Management:

SIEM tools are designed to collect and analyze log data generated throughout an organization's technology infrastructure, from host systems and applications to network and security devices. By centralizing this data, SIEM tools provide a comprehensive view of security events, allowing cybersecurity professionals to detect and respond to incidents promptly.

2. Real-Time Analysis and Correlation:

One of the key features of SIEM tools is their ability to perform real-time analysis and correlation of security events. This involves identifying patterns, anomalies, or trends in the data that may indicate security threats. SIEM tools leverage correlation rules and algorithms to connect seemingly unrelated events, providing a more accurate understanding of the security landscape.

3. Incident Detection and Response:

SIEM tools play a crucial role in incident detection and response. By continuously monitoring and analyzing security events, these tools can identify indicators of compromise and potential security incidents. Alerts generated by SIEM tools prompt cybersecurity professionals to investigate and respond to threats promptly, minimizing the impact of security breaches.

4. Log Management and Retention:

SIEM tools excel in log management, collecting and storing logs generated by various systems and devices. The retention of historical log data is essential for forensic analysis, compliance reporting, and identifying patterns of behavior over time. SIEM tools offer a centralized and structured approach to log management, ensuring that critical data is readily accessible.

Practical Applications of SIEM Tools in Cybersecurity

1. Threat Detection and Prevention:

   SIEM tools are instrumental in threat detection by monitoring for suspicious activities, unauthorized access attempts, or deviations from normal behavior. By correlating events from different sources, SIEM tools can identify sophisticated threats that may go unnoticed with isolated monitoring solutions. This proactive approach enhances an organization's ability to prevent security incidents.

2. Incident Investigation and Forensics:

   When a security incident occurs, SIEM tools provide a rich source of data for investigation and forensics. Cybersecurity professionals can trace the sequence of events, understand the scope and impact of a security incident, and gather evidence for further analysis. SIEM tools contribute to a comprehensive incident response strategy, aiding in the identification of root causes.

3. Compliance Monitoring and Reporting:

   Many industries and organizations are subject to regulatory compliance requirements. SIEM tools simplify compliance monitoring by collecting and organizing data needed for reporting. Whether it's the healthcare sector adhering to HIPAA, financial institutions complying with PCI DSS, or other industry-specific regulations, SIEM tools facilitate the generation of compliance reports.

4. User and Entity Behavior Analytics (UEBA):

   SIEM tools often integrate User and Entity Behavior Analytics (UEBA) to detect anomalous behavior patterns. UEBA functionality enhances the ability to identify insider threats, compromised accounts, or unusual activities that may indicate a security risk. By baselining normal behavior, SIEM tools with UEBA can quickly flag deviations for investigation.

Mastering SIEM Tools: A Strategic Approach

1. Understanding SIEM Architecture:

Start by understanding the architecture of SIEM tools. Explore how these tools collect, process, and store log data. Familiarize yourself with the components such as data collectors, event processors, and the user interface. This foundational knowledge forms the basis for effective utilization of SIEM tools.

2. Configuring Data Sources and Collectors:

SIEM tools rely on various data sources, including firewalls, antivirus solutions, servers, and more. Learn how to configure data collectors to gather logs from these sources. Understanding the nuances of collecting data ensures that the SIEM tool receives comprehensive information for analysis.

3. Creating Effective Correlation Rules:

Master the art of creating correlation rules. Correlation rules define conditions that, when met, trigger alerts or actions. Tailor these rules to the specific security needs of the organization. Effective correlation rules enhance the accuracy of threat detection and reduce false positives.

4. Incident Response and Investigation:

Practice incident response scenarios using SIEM tools. Simulate security incidents, investigate alerts generated by the SIEM, and formulate a response plan. This hands-on experience prepares cybersecurity professionals to effectively leverage SIEM tools during real-world incidents.

5. Integration with Other Security Tools:

SIEM tools are more powerful when integrated with other security solutions. Explore the integration capabilities of SIEM tools with firewalls, antivirus software, intrusion detection/prevention systems, and endpoint protection tools. This integration provides a holistic view of the security landscape.

6. Continuous Monitoring and Tuning:

SIEM tools require ongoing monitoring and tuning to adapt to changes in the organization's technology landscape. Regularly review and update correlation rules, ensure that new data sources are integrated, and fine-tune the system to minimize false positives. Continuous monitoring enhances the effectiveness of SIEM tools over time.

Challenges and Solutions in Implementing SIEM Tools

1. High Volume of Alerts:

SIEM tools can generate a high volume of alerts, leading to alert fatigue for cybersecurity professionals. To address this challenge, implement prioritization strategies, focus on critical alerts, and fine-tune correlation rules to reduce false positives. Automation and machine learning capabilities within modern SIEM tools can assist in intelligent alerting.

2. Resource Intensiveness:

Implementing and maintaining SIEM tools can be resource-intensive. Organizations may face challenges in terms of hardware requirements, storage capacity, and processing power. Cloud-based SIEM solutions and managed security services provide alternatives for resource-constrained environments.

3. Skill Gaps in Operations:

Operating SIEM tools effectively requires specific skills. Address skill gaps through training programs, certifications, and knowledge-sharing within the cybersecurity team. Leverage vendor documentation, online courses, and community resources to ensure that cybersecurity professionals are proficient in using SIEM tools.

Conclusion: SIEM Tools as Guardians of Cyber Resilience

In conclusion, mastering SIEM tools is not just about deploying a technology solution; it's about cultivating a strategic approach to cybersecurity. SIEM tools serve as the guardians of cyber resilience, providing organizations with the capability to detect, respond to, and mitigate security threats effectively. By understanding the role of SIEM tools, exploring their practical applications, and strategically approaching their implementation, cybersecurity professionals position themselves as stewards of digital defense. As the cyber landscape evolves, the mastery of SIEM tools becomes a cornerstone in the foundation of a robust cybersecurity career.

Hands-On Labs and Projects

In the ever-evolving realm of cybersecurity, theoretical knowledge alone is insufficient to navigate the complex landscape of threats and defences. Practical, hands-on experience is paramount to truly mastering cybersecurity tools and techniques. In this section, we will delve into the significance of hands-on labs and projects, exploring how they contribute to skill development, knowledge retention, and the strategic advancement of a cybersecurity career.

The Importance of Hands-On Experience

1. Bridge the Gap Between Theory and Practice:

Hands-on labs and projects serve as a bridge between theoretical understanding and practical application. While textbooks and courses provide a foundational understanding of cybersecurity concepts, engaging in hands-on activities allows individuals to translate that knowledge into real-world scenarios. This practical experience is invaluable in the dynamic and ever-changing field of cybersecurity.

2. Enhance Retention and Understanding:

The human brain retains information more effectively through experiential learning. Hands-on labs provide an immersive environment where cybersecurity professionals can apply theoretical knowledge, reinforcing their understanding of concepts. By actively working with cybersecurity tools, individuals solidify their grasp on how these tools function and how they can be strategically employed.

3. Develop Problem-Solving Skills:

Cybersecurity is inherently about problem-solving. Hands-on labs and projects present challenges that require individuals to apply critical thinking, analytical skills, and creativity. These practical exercises simulate real-world scenarios, empowering cybersecurity professionals to develop effective strategies for identifying and mitigating security threats.

4. Build Muscle Memory for Tools and Techniques:

Like any skill, proficiency in using cybersecurity tools comes with practice. Hands-on labs provide the opportunity to build muscle memory for using tools and executing techniques. Whether it's configuring a firewall, analyzing network traffic with Wireshark, or conducting penetration tests with Metasploit, repetitive practice enhances efficiency and proficiency.

Strategic Approach to Hands-On Labs and Projects

1. Define Learning Objectives:

Before embarking on hands-on labs and projects, clearly define your learning objectives. Identify specific skills, tools, or techniques you aim to master. This focused approach ensures that your hands-on activities align with your overall cybersecurity learning goals.

2. Curate a Diverse Set of Labs:

Cybersecurity encompasses a wide range of skills and knowledge areas, from network security to cryptography, penetration testing, and incident response. Curate a diverse set of hands-on labs and projects that cover various aspects of cybersecurity. This ensures a well-rounded skill set and a comprehensive understanding of the field.

3. Align with Industry Certifications:

Many industry-recognized certifications in cybersecurity, such as CompTIA Security+, Certified Ethical Hacker (CEH), and Offensive Security Certified Professional (OSCP), emphasize hands-on skills. Align your hands-on labs with the objectives of relevant certifications to prepare effectively for exams and validate your practical expertise.

4. Simulate Real-World Scenarios:

The effectiveness of hands-on labs lies in their ability to simulate real-world scenarios. Design projects that mimic common cybersecurity challenges and threat scenarios. This could include setting up a secure network, responding to a simulated incident, or conducting penetration tests in a controlled environment.

5. Progressive Complexity:

Structure your hands-on labs and projects in a progressive manner, starting with foundational exercises and gradually increasing complexity. This approach ensures a smooth learning curve, allowing individuals to build upon their skills incrementally. As proficiency grows, participants can tackle more challenging scenarios.

Examples of Hands-On Labs and Projects

1. Network Security Lab:

Create a network security lab where individuals can configure firewalls, implement intrusion detection/prevention systems, and monitor network traffic. Hands-on exercises can include setting up virtual networks, analyzing packet captures, and implementing access controls.

2. Penetration Testing Project:

Develop a penetration testing project that covers the entire process, from reconnaissance and scanning to exploitation and post-exploitation. Participants can use tools like Nmap, Metasploit, and Wireshark to identify vulnerabilities, launch simulated attacks, and assess the security posture of systems.

3. Incident Response Simulation:

Simulate an incident response scenario where participants must detect, analyse, and respond to a security incident. This hands-on project can involve investigating logs with SIEM tools, identifying indicators of compromise, and formulating a comprehensive incident response plan.

4. Cryptographic Protocols Lab:

Explore cryptographic protocols through a lab setting where participants implement encryption and decryption processes. Hands-on activities can include setting up secure communication channels, generating digital signatures, and understanding the practical applications of cryptographic algorithms.

5. Security Awareness Training Module:

Design a hands-on project focused on security awareness training. Participants can create and deliver a simulated security awareness program, covering topics such as phishing prevention, password hygiene, and social engineering awareness. This project not only reinforces technical skills but also emphasizes the human element of cybersecurity.

Challenges and Solutions in Hands-On Learning

1. Resource Constraints:

Setting up a dedicated hands-on lab may pose resource challenges, especially for individuals or organizations with limited hardware or budget constraints. Cloud-based platforms and virtualization technologies offer cost-effective solutions, enabling participants to access virtual labs from anywhere.

2. Time Management:

Balancing hands-on labs with other responsibilities can be a time-consuming endeavor. To address this challenge, establish a consistent schedule for hands-on activities. Short, focused sessions on a regular basis can be more effective than sporadic, lengthy sessions.

3. Access to Tools and Environments:

Some cybersecurity tools and environments may require specific permissions or licenses. To overcome this challenge, leverage open-source tools and platforms that are freely accessible. Many cybersecurity tools have community editions or offer trial versions for educational purposes.

Conclusion: Empowering Your Cybersecurity Journey through Hands-On Mastery

In conclusion, the mastery of cybersecurity tools is incomplete without the hands-on experience that bridges theory and practice. Hands-on labs and projects serve as the crucible in which theoretical knowledge transforms into practical expertise. By strategically approaching hands-on learning with defined objectives, diverse projects, and a progressive complexity, cybersecurity professionals can elevate their skills and readiness for the challenges of the cybersecurity landscape. The projects outlined here are starting points, and the key lies in customization—tailoring hands-on activities to your specific learning goals and career aspirations. Embrace the power of experiential learning, and let hands-on labs be the cornerstone of your journey toward becoming a proficient and strategic cybersecurity professional.

Creating Your Home Lab

In the dynamic and ever-evolving field of cybersecurity, a hands-on approach is indispensable for mastering the tools and techniques essential for success. While online courses and certifications provide a foundational understanding, creating your home lab offers a unique and immersive environment for practical learning. In this section, we will explore the importance of a home lab, the benefits it provides, and a strategic guide to creating and maximizing its potential for advancing your cybersecurity career.

The Significance of a Home Lab

1. Personalized Learning Environment:

A home lab provides a personalized learning environment tailored to your specific interests and career goals. Whether your focus is on penetration testing, network security, or incident response, you have the flexibility to curate a lab that aligns with your aspirations. This personalization fosters a deeper and more targeted learning experience.

2. Hands-On Skill Development:

The core advantage of a home lab lies in its hands-on nature. It allows you to actively engage with cybersecurity tools, simulate real-world scenarios, and develop practical skills. This direct experience is crucial for building muscle memory, enhancing proficiency, and gaining confidence in using tools that are integral to cybersecurity roles.

3. Cost-Effective Training Solution:

Creating a home lab is a cost-effective alternative to traditional training environments. While professional cybersecurity labs and training platforms may incur subscription fees, a home lab can be set up with relatively affordable hardware and open-source software. This financial accessibility makes it an ideal solution for those on a budget.

4. Continuous Learning Platform:

A home lab serves as a continuous learning platform that adapts to your evolving skill set. As you progress in your cybersecurity journey, you can expand and modify your home lab to explore advanced concepts, experiment with new tools, and stay current with emerging technologies. This adaptability ensures that your home lab remains a relevant and valuable resource throughout your career.

Strategic Guide to Creating Your Home Lab

1. Define Your Learning Objectives:

Begin by clearly defining your learning objectives. Identify the specific skills, tools, and areas of cybersecurity you want to focus on. Whether it's penetration testing, network security, or malware analysis, having a clear roadmap guides the setup and configuration of your home lab.

2. Select Hardware and Virtualization Platform:

Choose hardware that aligns with your budget and objectives. For a basic home lab, a powerful desktop or laptop with sufficient RAM and storage may suffice. Consider using virtualization platforms such as VMware, VirtualBox, or Hyper-V to create virtual machines, allowing you to simulate diverse environments on a single physical machine.

3. Curate a Toolset

Identify the cybersecurity tools you want to master and include them in your home lab environment. This could include tools for scanning and enumeration, penetration testing frameworks, network monitoring solutions, and incident response tools. Ensure that your toolset reflects the practical skills sought after in the cybersecurity industry.

4. Segment Your Lab:

For a comprehensive home lab experience, consider segmenting your environment into distinct zones. Create separate virtual networks for testing, development, and production. This segmentation enables you to simulate realistic scenarios, such as isolated networks and controlled attack surfaces, enhancing the authenticity of your hands-on exercises.

5. Experiment with Vulnerable Machines:

Include deliberately vulnerable machines in your home lab to practice exploitation and penetration testing. Platforms like Metasploitable, DVWA (Damn Vulnerable Web Application), and OWASP WebGoat provide a controlled environment for hands-on experimentation without the ethical concerns associated with unauthorized testing.

6. Simulate Real-World Scenarios:

Design projects that simulate real-world cybersecurity scenarios within your home lab. This could involve setting up a secure web application and attempting to identify and patch vulnerabilities, or creating a network with intentionally misconfigured settings for troubleshooting and securing. These projects offer practical insights and problem-solving opportunities.

7. Implement Security Controls:

Integrate security controls within your home lab to replicate the measures used in professional environments. This includes firewalls, intrusion detection/prevention systems, and log management solutions. Configuring and managing these controls enhances your understanding of defensive strategies and security best practices.

Benefits and Challenges of Creating Your Home Lab

Benefits:

1. Flexible Learning Schedule:

A home lab allows you to learn at your own pace and on your own schedule. You can experiment with cybersecurity tools and techniques without time constraints, making it conducive to both self-paced learning and continuous skill development.

2. Accessible Anytime, Anywhere:

Your home lab is accessible anytime, anywhere. Whether you're at home, traveling, or in a coffee shop, you can access your virtualized environment and continue your hands-on activities. This accessibility facilitates consistent and flexible learning, accommodating your lifestyle and commitments.

3. Customization and Personalization:

One of the primary advantages of a home lab is the ability to customize and personalize the environment to suit your learning goals. You have the freedom to choose the tools, technologies, and projects that align with your interests, ensuring a tailored and relevant learning experience.

Challenges:

1. Resource Limitations:

Home labs may face resource limitations, particularly in terms of hardware capabilities. This can impact the complexity and scale of simulations you can create. To address this, prioritize the most essential components and gradually expand your home lab as your resources allow.

2. Security Considerations:

Simulating real-world scenarios involves intentional exposure to vulnerabilities, which raises security considerations. Ensure that your home lab is isolated from your production network, implement proper security controls, and be mindful of the potential risks associated with experimenting with vulnerable machines.

3. Learning Curve:

Setting up and configuring a home lab, especially for those new to cybersecurity, may involve a learning curve. Understanding virtualization platforms, network configurations, and tool integrations requires patience and persistence. Leverage online resources, tutorials, and community support to navigate the initial challenges.

Conclusion: Empowering Your Journey with a Home Lab

In conclusion, creating your home lab is a strategic and empowering step in mastering cybersecurity tools and techniques. It provides a dedicated space for hands-on learning, skill development, and experimentation. By following a strategic guide, defining clear learning objectives, and embracing the benefits of customization, your home lab becomes a dynamic and evolving platform for advancing your cybersecurity career. As you embark on this hands-on journey, remember that the skills cultivated in your home lab are not just theoretical knowledge—They are the building blocks of practical expertise that will set you apart in the dynamic and competitive field of cybersecurity.

Real-world Simulations

In the pursuit of mastering cybersecurity tools, the integration of real-world simulations within hands-on labs and projects is a pivotal strategy. Simulations elevate practical learning experiences, providing a bridge between theoretical knowledge and the complex challenges faced in actual cybersecurity scenarios. In this section, we will explore the significance of real-world simulations, their benefits, and a strategic guide to incorporating them into your hands-on learning journey.

The Significance of Real-World Simulations

1. Bridging the Gap to Real-world Challenges:

Real-world simulations bring authenticity to your learning journey by replicating the challenges faced in actual cybersecurity scenarios. The gap between theory and practice is effectively narrowed as simulations immerse you in scenarios that mirror the complexities of the cyber landscape. This hands-on experience is invaluable for preparing cybersecurity professionals to navigate the unpredictable nature of cyber threats.

2. Developing Decision-making Skills:

Cybersecurity is not just about using tools; it involves making informed decisions in dynamic and high-pressure situations. Real-world simulations facilitate the development of decision-making skills by presenting scenarios that demand critical thinking, analysis, and rapid response. This aspect of hands-on learning is crucial for cultivating the instincts needed in cybersecurity roles.

3. Building Resilience in Adversarial Situations:

Cybersecurity professionals often operate in adversarial environments where threats are persistent and evolving. Real-world simulations expose you to scenarios where the stakes are high, and adversarial actors are actively trying to compromise systems. This exposure builds resilience, hones defensive strategies, and cultivates the ability to anticipate and respond effectively to cyber threats.

4. Practical Application of Tools in Context:

While mastering individual cybersecurity tools is essential, understanding how to apply them in real-world scenarios is equally crucial. Real-world simulations provide the context for using tools in a practical and meaningful way. This contextual understanding enhances your proficiency in tool usage and equips you with the skills needed to address diverse cybersecurity challenges.

Benefits of Real-World Simulations in Hands-On Learning

1. Holistic Skill Development:

Real-world simulations contribute to holistic skill development by integrating technical expertise with soft skills such as communication, teamwork, and decision-making. The multifaceted nature of simulations ensures that you are not only proficient in using tools but also adept at applying them within the broader context of cybersecurity operations.

2. Preparation for Incident Response:

Incident response is a critical aspect of cybersecurity, and real-world simulations provide a platform for honing these skills. Simulated incidents, ranging from data breaches to malware outbreaks, allow you to practice the end-to-end incident response process. This includes detection, analysis, containment, eradication, and recovery—preparing you for the challenges of handling real incidents.

3. Enhanced Critical Thinking:

Real-world simulations challenge your critical thinking abilities by presenting dynamic and evolving scenarios. Adapting to unforeseen circumstances, identifying the root cause of issues, and formulating effective response strategies require a high level of critical thinking. Simulations provide a safe yet realistic environment to cultivate and refine these skills.

4. Improved Communication and Collaboration:

Cybersecurity is a collaborative field where effective communication is paramount. Real-world simulations often involve teamwork, requiring participants to communicate findings, share insights, and coordinate responses. These collaborative experiences mirror the dynamics of real cybersecurity operations, fostering effective communication and teamwork skills.

Strategic Guide to Real-World Simulations in Hands-On Learning

1. Define Simulation Scenarios:

Begin by defining the scenarios you want to simulate. These scenarios should align with the cybersecurity skills you aim to develop and the specific challenges faced in your target role. Whether it's a simulated phishing attack, a ransomware incident, or a network intrusion, clarity in scenario definition is crucial.

2. Create a Realistic Environment:

Realism is key to effective simulations. Create an environment that mirrors the systems, networks, and technologies encountered in real-world cybersecurity operations. Use virtualization platforms to replicate diverse environments, ensuring that the simulation closely reflects the complexities of actual IT infrastructures.

3. Integrate Threat Intelligence:

Incorporate threat intelligence into your simulations to enhance authenticity. Threat intelligence adds a dynamic element to scenarios by introducing realistic threat actors, attack techniques, and indicators of compromise. This integration ensures that simulations are not only technically accurate but also aligned with the current threat landscape.

4. Include Response Coordination:

Simulations should extend beyond individual technical tasks to encompass response coordination. Introduce elements that require participants to collaborate, share information, and coordinate responses. This mirrors the reality of incident response, where effective teamwork and communication are integral to successful outcomes.

5. Capture and Analyze Metrics:

Implement mechanisms to capture and analyze metrics during simulations. Metrics can include response times, accuracy of threat detection, and effectiveness of containment measures. Analyzing these metrics provides valuable insights into performance, identifies areas for improvement, and facilitates a data-driven approach to refining simulation scenarios.

6. Debrief and Learning Review:

Following each simulation, conduct a thorough debrief and learning review session. This collaborative discussion allows participants to share their experiences, insights, and challenges. Identify lessons learned, discuss alternative approaches, and collectively analyze the effectiveness of the response. Debriefing is an essential component for continuous improvement.

Examples of Real-World Simulations

1. Phishing Simulation:

Simulate a phishing attack scenario where participants receive simulated phishing emails. The goal is to identify phishing attempts, report suspicious emails, and implement phishing awareness training measures. This simulation mirrors the real-world challenge of defending against social engineering attacks.

2. Ransomware Outbreak:

Create a simulation involving a ransomware outbreak within the simulated environment. Participants are tasked with detecting and containing the ransomware, identifying the entry point, and implementing recovery measures. This simulation provides hands-on experience in responding to a critical cybersecurity incident.

3. Network Intrusion Scenario:

Simulate a network intrusion scenario where participants must detect and respond to unauthorized access attempts. The simulation can involve analyzing network traffic, identifying indicators of compromise, and implementing measures to prevent further unauthorized access. This scenario enhances skills in network security and intrusion detection.

4. Incident Response Tabletop Exercise:

Conduct a tabletop exercise simulating a cybersecurity incident response scenario. Participants, representing different roles within the incident response team, collaborate to formulate and execute an incident response plan. This exercise enhances coordination, communication, and decision-making skills in a simulated real-world incident.

Challenges and Solutions in Real-World Simulations

1. Resource Intensity:

Creating realistic simulations may be resource-intensive, requiring diverse environments, threat intelligence feeds, and coordination mechanisms. To address this challenge, start with simpler simulations and gradually increase complexity. Leverage open-source threat intelligence feeds and collaborate with peers to share resources and expertise.

2. Balancing Realism and Safety:

Simulations must strike a balance between realism and safety. Introducing realistic threats is essential, but precautions must be taken to ensure that simulations do not inadvertently cause harm to systems or networks. Use controlled environments, isolate simulations from production systems, and prioritize safety in scenario design.

3. Overcoming Scripted Responses:

Participants may develop scripted responses if scenarios become predictable. To overcome this challenge, introduce dynamic elements, unexpected twists, and variations in each simulation. Encourage participants to think on their feet, adapt to evolving situations, and avoid relying on memorized responses.

Conclusion: Elevating Mastery Through Real-World Simulations

In conclusion, real-world simulations are the catalyst for elevating mastery in cybersecurity tools and techniques. The strategic integration of simulations within hands-on labs and projects transforms theoretical knowledge into practical expertise. By embracing the authenticity of real-world scenarios, cybersecurity professionals are better equipped to navigate the complexities of the cyber landscape. The examples and strategic guide provided here serve as a blueprint for creating impactful simulations that align with your learning objectives and career aspirations. As you embark on this hands-on journey, let real-world simulations be the cornerstone of your path to becoming a proficient and strategic cybersecurity professional.

Chapter 6: Certifications as Milestones

Entry-Level Certifications

CompTIA Security+

In the dynamic landscape of cybersecurity, certifications serve as crucial milestones in one's career journey. They validate skills, enhance credibility, and open doors to new opportunities. For individuals entering the field, securing entry-level certifications is a strategic starting point. In this section, we will explore the significance of entry-level certifications, focusing on the renowned CompTIA Security+ certification and its role in shaping the foundation of a cybersecurity career.

The Significance of Entry-Level Certifications

1. Building a Solid Foundation:

Entry-level certifications play a pivotal role in building a solid foundation for a career in cybersecurity. These certifications are designed to cover fundamental concepts, terminology, and skills that are universally applicable across various cybersecurity domains. they provide a baseline understanding that serves as a springboard for more advanced certifications and specialized roles.

2. Industry Recognition and Credibility:

Certifications offer industry-recognized validation of skills and knowledge. For individuals entering the cybersecurity field, earning entry-level certifications signals to employers that they possess the foundational understanding necessary for entry-level roles. This recognition enhances credibility and increases the likelihood of securing opportunities in a competitive job market.

3. Pathway to Specialization:

Entry-level certifications serve as a pathway to specialization within cybersecurity. As individuals gain foundational knowledge, they can explore specific domains of interest and pursue advanced certifications tailored to those areas. This progression allows for a strategic and structured career development plan, aligning certifications with evolving career goals.

4. Employability and Career Advancement:

Entry-level certifications significantly contribute to employability. Employers often use certifications as criteria for screening candidates, and possessing relevant certifications can give individuals a competitive edge. Furthermore, entry-level certifications lay the groundwork for career advancement by providing the knowledge necessary for handling more complex responsibilities as one gains experience.

CompTIA Security+: An Overview

1. Introduction to CompTIA Security+:

CompTIA Security+ is a globally recognized entry-level certification that focuses on foundational cybersecurity skills. It is vendor-neutral, making it applicable across different cybersecurity environments and technologies. Security+ is designed for individuals with two years of work experience in IT with a security focus or equivalent knowledge, making it an ideal starting point for those entering the field.

2. Exam Objectives and Coverage:

The Security+ certification covers a broad range of topics, ensuring that certified professionals have a well-rounded understanding of cybersecurity principles. Key exam objectives include:

1. Threats, Attacks, and Vulnerabilities
2. Technologies and Tools
3. Architecture and Design
4. Identity and Access Management
5. Risk Management
6. Cryptography and Public Key Infrastructure (PKI)

3. Vendor-Neutral Approach:

One of the strengths of CompTIA Security+ is its vendor-neutral approach. This means that the certification is not tied to a specific technology or product. Instead, it focuses on core cybersecurity concepts and principles that are applicable across diverse IT environments. This neutrality is advantageous for individuals seeking flexibility in their career paths.

4. Suitability for Entry-Level Professionals:

CompTIA Security+ is well-suited for entry-level professionals as it covers foundational cybersecurity knowledge. The certification helps individuals establish a baseline understanding of security concepts, terminology, and best practices. It serves as a stepping stone for those aiming to pursue more advanced certifications and specialized roles in the future.

Benefits of CompTIA Security+ for Entry-Level Professionals

1. Foundational Knowledge:

Security+ provides foundational knowledge essential for understanding the fundamentals of cybersecurity. This includes threat landscapes, security technologies, risk management, and cryptographic principles. The certification ensures that entry-level professionals have a comprehensive understanding of key concepts.

2. Global Recognition:

CompTIA Security+ is globally recognized, making it valuable for entry-level professionals seeking opportunities beyond regional boundaries. The certification is acknowledged by employers worldwide, contributing to the portability of skills and enhancing the employability of certified individuals on a global scale.

3. Career Flexibility:

The vendor-neutral nature of Security+ offers career flexibility. Entry-level professionals can use the certification as a foundation to explore various cybersecurity domains without being tied to specific technologies. This flexibility is beneficial for those who may be considering different career paths within the broader field of cybersecurity.

4. Industry Validation:

Security+ is widely recognized and respected within the cybersecurity industry. Achieving this certification validates an individual's commitment to cybersecurity excellence and signifies their readiness for entry-level roles. Employers often view Security+ as a reliable indicator of foundational cybersecurity knowledge.

Strategic Approach to CompTIA Security+ Certification

1. Assessing Prerequisites and Readiness:

Before pursuing CompTIA Security+, individuals should assess their readiness and ensure they meet the prerequisites. While there is no strict prerequisite for taking the exam, having a foundational understanding of IT concepts and some work experience can contribute to a more successful exam experience.

2. Creating a Study Plan:

Developing a structured study plan is essential for success. Break down the exam objectives into manageable sections and allocate time for each. Utilize a combination of study materials, including official CompTIA resources, textbooks, online courses, and practice exams. This diversified approach enhances comprehension and retention of the material.

3. Hands-On Practice:

Security+ is not just about theoretical knowledge; it also assesses practical skills. Incorporate hands-on practice by setting up a home lab or utilizing virtual environments. Experimenting with cybersecurity tools and concepts in a practical setting reinforces theoretical learning and enhances overall readiness for the exam.

4. Engaging with the Community:

Joining online forums, discussion groups, and community platforms dedicated to CompTIA Security+ can provide valuable insights and support. Engaging with the community allows individuals to share experiences, seek advice, and gain a broader perspective on the certification process. Learning from the experiences of others can contribute to a more well-rounded preparation.

Challenges and Solutions in CompTIA Security+ Preparation

1. Balancing Theory and Practice:

Security+ requires a balance between theoretical understanding and practical application. To address this challenge, allocate sufficient time for hands-on practice alongside theoretical study. Practical exercises, simulations, and real-world scenarios contribute to a more comprehensive preparation.

2. Managing Exam Anxiety:

Exam anxiety is a common challenge. To mitigate this, simulate exam conditions during practice sessions, take timed practice exams, and focus on time management. Additionally, adopting relaxation techniques and maintaining a positive mindset can contribute to a calmer and more focused exam experience.

3. Staying Updated with Exam Objectives:

CompTIA certifications are periodically updated to reflect changes in the cybersecurity landscape. Stay informed about updates to the Security+ exam objectives and adjust study materials accordingly. CompTIA's official website is a reliable source for the latest exam information and resources.

Conclusion: Launching Your Cybersecurity Career with CompTIA Security+

In conclusion, CompTIA Security+ stands as a cornerstone for individuals embarking on a cybersecurity career journey. This entry-level certification provides a solid foundation, industry recognition, and a pathway to specialization within the field. By strategically approaching Security+ with a well-defined study plan, hands-on practice, and community engagement, entry-level professionals can enhance their readiness, credibility, and employability. CompTIA Security+ is not just a certification; it is a milestone that marks the beginning of a rewarding and dynamic career in cybersecurity. As you embark on this journey, let Security+ be the key that unlocks the doors to a world of possibilities in the ever-evolving realm of cybersecurity.

Certified Ethical Hacker (CEH)

In the realm of cybersecurity, certifications serve as milestones that validate skills, demonstrate expertise, and provide a clear pathway for career progression. For those aspiring to enter the field, entry-level certifications are essential stepping stones that establish a strong foundation. Among these certifications, the Certified Ethical Hacker (CEH) stands out as a key credential, signaling a commitment to ethical hacking and penetration testing. In this section, we will delve into the significance of entry-level certifications, with a focus on the Certified Ethical Hacker and its role in shaping the cybersecurity landscape.

The Significance of Entry-Level Certifications

1. Foundational Knowledge and Skills:

Entry-level certifications are instrumental in providing foundational knowledge and skills that are fundamental to a career in cybersecurity. These certifications cover essential concepts, best practices, and tools, offering a well-rounded understanding of the cybersecurity landscape. For individuals entering the field, these certifications serve as the bedrock upon which advanced skills can be built.

2. Industry Recognition and Employability:

Certifications enjoy widespread industry recognition, providing a standardized measure of an individual's proficiency in specific areas of cybersecurity. This recognition enhances employability by signaling to employers that candidates have attained a certain level of competence. In a competitive job market, possessing entry-level certifications can give candidates a distinct advantage.

3. Career Pathway and Specialization:

Entry-level certifications pave the way for career progression and specialization. As professionals gain experience and expertise, they can pursue advanced certifications that align with their specific interests and career goals. This strategic progression allows individuals to tailor their skill set to the evolving demands of the cybersecurity landscape.

4. Validation of Ethical Practices:

Many entry-level certifications, including the CEH, emphasize ethical practices and responsible conduct in the cybersecurity domain. This validation is crucial for professionals who aspire to engage in ethical hacking and penetration testing roles. It not only establishes a commitment to ethical behavior but also builds trust with employers and clients.

Certified Ethical Hacker (CEH): An Overview

1. Introduction to CEH:

The Certified Ethical Hacker (CEH) certification is a globally recognized credential that focuses on ethical hacking and penetration testing. Offered by the EC-Council, CEH is designed for individuals who want to demonstrate their proficiency in identifying and fixing vulnerabilities in computer systems and networks.

2. Exam Objectives and Coverage:

The CEH exam covers a comprehensive range of topics related to ethical hacking and penetration testing. Key exam objectives include:

1. Ethical hacking fundamentals
2. Foot printing and reconnaissance
3. Scanning networks
4. Enumeration
5. System hacking
6. Malware threats
7. Sniffing
8. Social engineering
9. Web application hacking
10. Wireless network hacking
11. Cryptography

3. Practical Focus and Hands-On Experience:

One distinguishing feature of the CEH certification is its practical focus. The exam assesses not only theoretical knowledge but also hands-on skills. CEH-certified professionals are expected to demonstrate their ability to identify and exploit vulnerabilities in a controlled and ethical manner. This practical orientation ensures that certified individuals are well-prepared for real-world scenarios.

4. Ethical Hacking and Penetration Testing:

CEH places a strong emphasis on ethical hacking and penetration testing, aligning with industry demands for professionals who can proactively identify and address security vulnerabilities. Certified Ethical Hackers are equipped to simulate cyberattacks, assess security postures, and provide recommendations for strengthening defenses. This skill set is invaluable in enhancing overall cybersecurity resilience.

Benefits of CEH for Entry-Level Professionals

1. Comprehensive Skill Set:

CEH equips entry-level professionals with a comprehensive skill set covering various aspects of ethical hacking and penetration testing. This includes the ability to conduct vulnerability assessments, perform penetration tests, and identify security weaknesses across different domains. The certification ensures a well-rounded understanding of offensive security practices.

2. Global Recognition and Credibility:

CEH enjoys global recognition and credibility within the cybersecurity community. Certified Ethical Hackers are recognized as professionals who adhere to ethical standards and possess the skills needed to assess and fortify cybersecurity defences. This recognition enhances the credibility of entry-level professionals seeking to establish themselves in the field.

3. Practical Experience in Cybersecurity:

The hands-on nature of CEH ensures that entry-level professionals gain practical experience in cybersecurity. Through simulated exercises and real-world scenarios, individuals develop the ability to identify vulnerabilities, exploit weaknesses, and recommend remediation measures. This practical exposure is invaluable for building confidence and competence in cybersecurity roles.

4. Pathway to Specialized Roles:

CEH serves as a pathway to specialized roles within the cybersecurity domain. Entry-level professionals who attain the CEH certification can choose to specialize in areas such as penetration testing, vulnerability assessment, or ethical hacking. The certification provides a foundation upon which professionals can build expertise in their chosen niche.

Strategic Approach to CEH Certification

1. Preparation and Study Resources:

A strategic approach to CEH certification begins with thorough preparation. Utilize a combination of study resources, including official EC-Council materials, textbooks, online courses, and practice exams. Familiarize yourself with the exam objectives and allocate dedicated time to each topic. Engage with the CEH community to gain insights and tips from those who have successfully completed the certification.

2. Hands-On Labs and Practical Exercises:

Given the practical focus of CEH, hands-on labs and practical exercises are essential components of preparation. Set up a home lab or leverage virtual environments to simulate real-world scenarios. Practice identifying vulnerabilities, conducting penetration tests, and applying ethical hacking techniques. This hands-on experience enhances both technical skills and problem-solving capabilities.

3. Stay Current with Industry Trends:

The field of cybersecurity is dynamic, with new threats and technologies emerging regularly. Stay current with industry trends, updates, and evolving cybersecurity challenges. EC-Council periodically updates the CEH certification to reflect these changes, and staying informed ensures that your knowledge remains relevant and aligned with the latest industry developments.

4. Engage with the Ethical Hacking Community:

Joining the ethical hacking community is a strategic step in your CEH certification journey. Online forums, discussion groups, and community platforms provide opportunities to connect with experienced professionals, share insights, and seek advice. Engaging with the community enhances your understanding of ethical hacking practices and fosters a collaborative learning environment.

Challenges and Solutions in CEH Preparation

1. Managing the Volume of Content:

The breadth of topics covered in the CEH certification can be overwhelming. To address this challenge, break down the content into manageable sections and create a study plan. Focus on one topic at a time, allocate sufficient study time, and use a variety of resources to reinforce your understanding.

2. Balancing Theory and Practice:

Achieving a balance between theoretical knowledge and practical skills is crucial for CEH success. To overcome this challenge, ensure that your preparation includes hands-on labs and practical exercises. Apply theoretical concepts in a simulated environment to reinforce your understanding and develop practical proficiency.

3. Time Management During the Exam:

The CEH exam is time-sensitive, requiring effective time management. To address this challenge, practice taking timed exams and simulate exam conditions during your preparation. Develop strategies for allocating time to different sections of the exam, ensuring that you can complete all tasks within the allotted timeframe.

Conclusion: Paving the Way to Ethical Hacking Excellence

In conclusion, the Certified Ethical Hacker (CEH) certification serves as a gateway for entry-level professionals entering the dynamic field of cybersecurity. By emphasizing ethical hacking, penetration testing, and practical skills, CEH equips individuals with the tools needed to proactively address cybersecurity challenges. The benefits of a comprehensive skill set, global recognition, and a pathway to specialized roles make CEH a strategic choice for those seeking to launch their careers in ethical hacking. Through a strategic approach to preparation, hands-on experience, and community engagement, entry-level professionals can position themselves as ethical hacking experts, contributing to the overall security of digital ecosystems. As you embark on the CEH certification journey, let it be a transformative milestone that propels you towards excellence in ethical hacking and a fulfilling career in the ever-evolving landscape of cybersecurity.

Certified Information Systems Security Professional (CISSP)

As cybersecurity professionals advance in their careers, the pursuit of advanced certifications becomes a strategic imperative. These certifications not only validate expertise but also signify a commitment to mastering complex cybersecurity domains. Among the pantheon of advanced certifications, the Certified Information Systems Security Professional (CISSP) stands as a beacon of excellence. In this section, we will delve into the significance of advanced certifications, focusing on the CISSP and its role in shaping the trajectory of cybersecurity professionals seeking to attain the highest echelons of mastery.

The Significance of Advanced Certifications

1. Elevating Expertise to Mastery:

Advanced certifications are a testament to the elevation of expertise to mastery. They go beyond foundational knowledge, demanding a deep understanding and application of complex cybersecurity concepts. Achieving advanced certifications signals not only technical proficiency but also the ability to strategize, lead, and make informed decisions in the face of evolving cyber threats.

2. Leadership and Strategic Impact:

Advanced certifications are often associated with leadership roles in cybersecurity. These certifications are tailored to professionals who aspire to influence strategic decisions, shape cybersecurity policies, and lead organizations in their cybersecurity endeavors. The attainment of advanced certifications positions individuals to have a meaningful impact on the strategic direction of cybersecurity initiatives.

3. Recognition Within the Industry:

Within the cybersecurity industry, advanced certifications are recognized as hallmarks of excellence. Professionals who hold these certifications are viewed as authoritative figures who have demonstrated a mastery of their craft. This recognition extends beyond individual accomplishments and contributes to the collective reputation of organizations that employ such highly certified professionals.

4. Adaptability to Diverse Security Domains:

Advanced certifications often cover a wide range of security domains, reflecting the complex and multifaceted nature of modern cybersecurity. Professionals holding these certifications demonstrate the ability to adapt to diverse challenges, whether in risk management, governance, cryptography, or security architecture. This adaptability is a key characteristic of seasoned cybersecurity experts.

Certified Information Systems Security Professional (CISSP): An Overview

1. Introduction to CISSP:

The Certified Information Systems Security Professional (CISSP) is a premier advanced certification offered by (ISC)². CISSP is designed for cybersecurity professionals with significant experience in the field and aims to validate their expertise in various security domains. It is widely regarded as one of the most prestigious certifications in the cybersecurity industry.

2. Common Body of Knowledge (CBK) Domains:

The CISSP exam is based on a Common Body of Knowledge (CBK) that spans eight security domains. These domains cover the breadth and depth of cybersecurity, ensuring that CISSP-certified professionals possess a comprehensive understanding of key concepts. The domains include:

1. Security and Risk Management
2. Asset Security
3. Security Architecture and Engineering
4. Communication and Network Security
5. Identity and Access Management (IAM)
6. Security Assessment and Testing
7. Security Operations
8. Software Development Security

3. Experience Requirements:

One distinguishing feature of CISSP is its experience requirements. Candidates must have a minimum of five years of cumulative, paid, full-time work experience in two or more of the eight domains covered in the CISSP CBK. A relevant four-year college degree or other approved credential can substitute for one year of the required experience.

4. Endorsement and Adherence to Code of Ethics:

CISSP candidates must be endorsed by an existing (ISC)² certified professional who can attest to their professional experience and qualifications. Additionally, CISSP-certified professionals are bound by a Code of Ethics that emphasizes integrity, confidentiality, and a commitment to advancing and protecting the cybersecurity profession.

Benefits of CISSP for Cybersecurity Professionals

1. Gold Standard of Cybersecurity Certification:

CISSP is widely regarded as the gold standard of cybersecurity certifications. Achieving CISSP certification is a prestigious accomplishment that signals to the industry a high level of expertise and commitment to ethical practices. CISSP-certified professionals are recognized as leaders and experts in the field.

2. Global Recognition and Career Opportunities:

CISSP enjoys global recognition, opening doors to career opportunities on an international scale. Organizations value CISSP certification when seeking leaders and decision-makers in cybersecurity. CISSP-certified professionals are well-positioned for roles such as Chief Information Security Officer (CISO), security consultant, and other leadership positions.

3. Comprehensive Coverage of Security Domains:

CISSP's comprehensive coverage of security domains ensures that certified professionals possess a holistic understanding of cybersecurity. From risk management to software development security, CISSP equips individuals to address the diverse challenges faced by organizations in today's complex threat landscape.

4. Community Engagement and Continued Learning:

CISSP certification encourages community engagement and continued learning. CISSP-certified professionals are part of a global community of cybersecurity experts facilitated by (ISC)². This community provides opportunities for networking, knowledge sharing, and staying abreast of the latest developments in the ever-evolving field of cybersecurity.

Strategic Approach to CISSP Certification

1. Assessing Readiness and Experience:

Before pursuing CISSP certification, individuals should assess their readiness and ensure they meet the experience requirements. CISSP is designed for seasoned professionals, and candidates should have substantial experience in multiple security domains. Evaluate your professional background and determine if you have the requisite experience.

2. Developing a Study Plan:

CISSP requires a disciplined and structured study approach. Develop a comprehensive study plan that aligns with the eight CISSP domains. Allocate dedicated time to each domain, utilize official (ISC)² resources, textbooks, online courses, and practice exams. CISSP preparation is not just about passing an exam; it's about deeply understanding the principles and practices of cybersecurity.

3. Engaging in Practical Application:

CISSP certification is not only about theoretical knowledge but also practical application. Draw on your real-world experiences to enhance your understanding of CISSP concepts. Relate the CISSP domains to your professional experiences and consider how the principles covered in CISSP can be applied to address challenges in your current or previous roles.

4. Seeking Mentorship and Community Involvement:

CISSP candidates can benefit from mentorship and community involvement. Seek guidance from CISSP-certified professionals who can provide insights into the certification process and share their experiences. Engage with the (ISC)² community, attend events, and participate in forums to connect with professionals who have successfully navigated the CISSP journey.

Challenges and Solutions in CISSP Preparation

1. Balancing Work and Study:

Balancing work responsibilities with CISSP preparation can be challenging. To address this, create a realistic study schedule that aligns with your work commitments. Break down your study plan into manageable sections and consistently dedicate focused time to CISSP preparation.

2. Navigating the Depth of Domains:

CISSP's coverage of eight domains requires in-depth understanding. To navigate the depth of domains, prioritize domains based on your existing knowledge and experience. Devote more time to areas where you may have less familiarity and leverage your strengths in domains where you already excel.

3. Maintaining Motivation Throughout the Process:

CISSP preparation is a rigorous process that requires sustained motivation. To maintain motivation, set realistic goals, celebrate milestones, and visualize the long-term benefits of CISSP certification. Connect with study groups or accountability partners to stay motivated and share the journey with like-minded individuals.

Conclusion: Attaining the Pinnacle of Cybersecurity Excellence

In conclusion, the Certified Information Systems Security Professional (CISSP) certification represents the pinnacle of cybersecurity excellence. For seasoned professionals seeking to ascend to leadership roles and make a significant impact on the industry, CISSP is not just a certification; it's a validation of mastery across diverse security domains. The strategic pursuit of CISSP requires a combination of experience, disciplined preparation, practical application, and community engagement. As you embark on the CISSP certification journey, let it be a transformative milestone that propels you to the forefront of cybersecurity leadership. The benefits of global recognition, comprehensive knowledge, and community involvement position CISSP-certified professionals as influential leaders in safeguarding the digital landscape. May the CISSP certification be the key that unlocks new heights in your cybersecurity career and establishes you as a beacon of excellence in the ever-evolving world of cybersecurity.

Offensive Security Certified Professional (OSCP)

In the dynamic and ever-evolving field of cybersecurity, advanced certifications serve as beacons of excellence, indicating a profound mastery of specialized domains. Among these, the Offensive Security Certified Professional (OSCP) stands out as a testament to hands-on skills and proficiency in offensive security practices. This section explores the significance of advanced certifications, focusing on the OSCP and its pivotal role in shaping the careers of cybersecurity professionals seeking mastery in offensive security.

The Significance of Advanced Certifications

1. Mastery of Specialized Domains:

Advanced certifications signify a mastery of specialized domains within cybersecurity. Professionals who attain these certifications demonstrate a deep understanding and practical application of advanced concepts and techniques. This level of expertise positions individuals as leaders and specialists in their chosen areas, contributing significantly to the cybersecurity landscape.

2. Practical Application of Knowledge:

Unlike entry-level certifications that often assess theoretical knowledge, advanced certifications place a strong emphasis on practical application. Professionals holding advanced certifications, such as the OSCP, are adept at applying their knowledge in real-world scenarios. This practical focus ensures that certified individuals are well-equipped to address complex cybersecurity challenges.

3. Industry Recognition and Trust:

Advanced certifications enjoy widespread industry recognition and trust. Employers, clients, and peers view professionals with advanced certifications as trusted experts who can navigate and mitigate sophisticated cyber threats. The attainment of advanced certifications elevates an individual's credibility within the cybersecurity community.

4. Strategic Career Advancement:

Advanced certifications play a strategic role in career advancement. They open the doors to higher-level positions, leadership roles, and specialized niches within cybersecurity. Professionals with advanced certifications are often sought after for their ability to provide strategic insights, lead complex projects, and make critical decisions in the ever-evolving landscape of cyber threats.

Offensive Security Certified Professional (OSCP)

An Overview

1. Introduction to OSCP:

The Offensive Security Certified Professional (OSCP) certification is offered by Offensive Security, a leading provider of hands-on cybersecurity training and certifications. OSCP is renowned for its practical approach, focusing on the skills required for ethical hacking and penetration testing. It is designed for professionals who want to master the art of offensive security.

2. Hands-On Labs and Real-World Challenges:

One of the distinctive features of OSCP is its hands-on approach. The certification requires candidates to navigate through a series of labs and real-world challenges in a controlled environment. This practical experience goes beyond theoretical knowledge, ensuring that OSCP-certified professionals are adept at identifying and exploiting vulnerabilities.

3. 24-Hour Certification Exam:

OSCP culminates in a 24-hour hands-on certification exam, where candidates must demonstrate their ability to compromise a series of machines within a specified time frame. The exam mirrors real-world scenarios and assesses not only technical skills but also perseverance, time management, and problem-solving abilities. Successful completion of the exam is a testament to a candidate's practical proficiency.

4. Focus on Methodology and Creativity:

OSCP places a strong emphasis on methodology and creativity. Candidates are encouraged to develop their approach to solving challenges, simulating the mindset of a real-world attacker. This focus on creativity ensures that OSCP-certified professionals can think outside the box and adapt to novel and unforeseen security scenarios.

Benefits of OSCP for Cybersecurity Professionals

1. Practical Proficiency in Penetration Testing:

OSCP provides practical proficiency in penetration testing, equipping professionals with the skills needed to identify, exploit, and secure vulnerabilities. The hands-on labs and real-world challenges simulate actual scenarios, ensuring that OSCP-certified individuals are well-prepared for the complexities of offensive security practices.

2. Demonstrable Skill Set:

OSCP certification is a tangible demonstration of a candidate's skill set. The certification is not solely based on theoretical knowledge but on the ability to practically apply that knowledge in a live environment. OSCP-certified professionals have a demonstrable track record of hands-on expertise, making them valuable assets in the cybersecurity workforce.

3. Versatility in Offensive Security Practices:

OSCP fosters versatility in offensive security practices. Professionals holding this certification are well-versed in various penetration testing techniques, methodologies, and tools. This versatility enables OSCP-certified individuals to adapt to diverse environments and effectively address the unique challenges presented by different systems and networks.

4. Recognition Within the Security Community:

OSCP is widely recognized within the security community as a hallmark of excellence in penetration testing. Achieving OSCP certification signifies a commitment to continuous learning, practical skills development, and ethical hacking practices. OSCP-certified professionals are respected members of the cybersecurity community, often sought after for their expertise.

Strategic Approach to OSCP Certification

1. Building a Foundation in Networking and Security:

Before pursuing OSCP certification, it is crucial to build a solid foundation in networking and security fundamentals. Proficiency in areas such as TCP/IP, network protocols, and basic security concepts lays the groundwork for success in OSCP. Consider obtaining foundational certifications or practical experience in these areas.

2. Engaging in Practical Labs and Challenges:

OSCP's emphasis on practical application makes engaging in hands-on labs and challenges essential for success. Prioritize practical experience over theoretical knowledge, and actively participate in labs that simulate real-world scenarios. Platforms and environments that provide vulnerable machines for exploitation can enhance your skills in preparation for OSCP.

3. Developing a Methodical Approach:

OSCP rewards a methodical and systematic approach to problem-solving. Develop a structured methodology for penetration testing, encompassing reconnaissance, enumeration, vulnerability analysis, exploitation, and post-exploitation activities. Having a well-defined approach not only enhances efficiency but also contributes to success in the OSCP exam.

4. Time Management and Persistence:

The OSCP certification exam spans 24 hours, requiring effective time management and persistence. Practice time management during your preparation by simulating exam conditions. Develop strategies for prioritizing tasks and maintaining focus throughout extended periods. Cultivate persistence, as the exam may present challenges that require tenacity to overcome.

Challenges and Solutions in OSCP Preparation

1. Overcoming the Learning Curve:

OSCP is known for its steep learning curve, which can be challenging for some candidates. To overcome this, take a systematic approach to learning, starting with foundational concepts before delving into more advanced topics. Break down complex challenges into manageable parts, and gradually build your skills through hands-on practice.

2. Dealing with Exam Anxiety:

The 24-hour duration of the OSCP exam can induce anxiety in some candidates. To address exam anxiety, practice taking extended-length exams under simulated conditions. Develop relaxation techniques to manage stress during the exam. Remember that persistence and a methodical approach can contribute to success even in challenging situations.

3. Balancing Work and Study:

Balancing work commitments with OSCP preparation can be demanding. To manage this, create a realistic study schedule that accommodates your work responsibilities. Prioritize areas where you may need more focus and allocate dedicated time to hands-on labs. Seek support from your employer if possible, emphasizing the mutual benefits of your OSCP certification.

Conclusion: Mastering Offensive Security with OSCP

In conclusion, the Offensive Security Certified Professional (OSCP) certification stands as a pinnacle in the realm of offensive security. For cybersecurity professionals seeking to master the art of ethical hacking and penetration testing, OSCP represents more than a certification—it is a badge of practical proficiency, creativity, and resilience. The strategic pursuit of OSCP requires a blend of foundational knowledge, practical labs, methodical approaches, and a commitment to continuous learning. As you embark on the OSCP certification journey, let it be a transformative milestone that propels you into the elite ranks of offensive security experts. The benefits of practical proficiency, versatility, and recognition within the cybersecurity community position OSCP-certified professionals as invaluable assets in the ongoing battle against cyber threats. May the OSCP certification be the key that unlocks new dimensions in your cybersecurity career, allowing you to navigate and secure the digital landscape with unparalleled expertise and skill.

Chapter 7: Gaining Practical Experience

Internships and Entry-Level Positions

In the dynamic and rapidly evolving field of cybersecurity, gaining practical experience is paramount for launching a successful career. Internships and entry-level positions serve as invaluable steppingstones for individuals looking to bridge the gap between theoretical knowledge and real-world application. In this chapter, we will explore the significance of internships and entry-level positions in cybersecurity and provide strategic insights on how to maximize these opportunities for professional growth.

The Crucial Role of Practical Experience in Cybersecurity

1. Bridging the Gap between Theory and Practice

While academic programs and certifications provide a foundational understanding of cybersecurity concepts, practical experience is the bridge that connects theory to real-world application. Internships and entry-level positions offer individuals the opportunity to apply their knowledge in dynamic, hands-on scenarios, gaining a deeper understanding of the complexities of cybersecurity.

2. Exposure to Diverse Cybersecurity Environments:

Practical experience exposes individuals to diverse cybersecurity environments. Whether working in a corporate setting, government agency, or cybersecurity firm, interns and entry-level professionals encounter unique challenges and threat landscapes. This exposure broadens their perspectives and equips them with the adaptability needed to navigate the multifaceted world of cybersecurity.

3. Development of Critical Soft Skills:

Beyond technical proficiency, internships and entry-level positions play a crucial role in developing soft skills essential for success in cybersecurity. These include communication, teamwork, problem-solving, and the ability to effectively convey complex technical concepts to non-technical stakeholders. Such skills are integral to building a well-rounded cybersecurity professional.

4. Establishing a Professional Network:

Practical experience provides the opportunity to establish a professional network within the cybersecurity community. Interacting with experienced professionals, mentors, and peers during internships and entry-level positions not only enhances knowledge sharing but also opens doors to future collaboration, mentorship, and job opportunities.

The Strategic Significance of Internships in Cybersecurity

1. Hands-On Learning in Real-World Scenarios:

Internships offer a unique environment for hands-on learning in real-world cybersecurity scenarios. Working on actual projects, responding to incidents, and collaborating with seasoned professionals provide interns with a practical understanding of how cybersecurity principles are applied in the field.

2. Exposure to Different Cybersecurity Roles:

Internships expose individuals to a variety of cybersecurity roles, allowing them to explore and identify areas of interest and specialization. Whether involved in vulnerability assessments, incident response, or security policy development, interns can gain insights into different facets of cybersecurity and make informed decisions about their career paths.

3. Building a Portfolio of Practical Achievements:

Internships enable individuals to build a portfolio of practical achievements. This can include successful completion of projects, contributions to security initiatives, and tangible outcomes that demonstrate their impact. A robust portfolio becomes a powerful asset when seeking entry-level positions or advancing to more specialized roles within the cybersecurity field.

4. Cultivating Mentorship and Guidance:

Internships provide a valuable opportunity to cultivate mentorship and guidance from experienced professionals. Establishing relationships with mentors enables interns to tap into the wealth of knowledge and experience within the cybersecurity community. Mentorship not only accelerates learning but also provides invaluable insights into career development.

Strategic Approaches to Securing Cybersecurity Internships

1. Researching and Targeting Opportunities:

A strategic approach to securing a cybersecurity internship begins with thorough research and targeting of opportunities. Identify organizations, companies, or government agencies that align with your career goals. Research their cybersecurity programs, initiatives, and internship offerings. Tailor your applications to demonstrate a genuine interest in their specific cybersecurity focus areas.

2. Showcasing Relevant Skills and Projects:

When applying for cybersecurity internships, showcase relevant skills and projects on your resume and in your application. Highlight any academic projects, certifications, or personal initiatives that demonstrate your practical knowledge and passion for cybersecurity. This not only sets you apart but also provides evidence of your commitment to the field.

3. Networking and Informational Interviews:

Networking plays a pivotal role in securing cybersecurity internships. Attend industry events, conferences, and online forums to connect with professionals in the field. Request informational interviews with individuals working in cybersecurity roles of interest. This proactive approach not only expands your network but also provides insights into potential internship opportunities.

4. Preparing for Technical Interviews:

Many cybersecurity internships involve technical interviews to assess candidates' practical skills. Prepare for these interviews by reviewing common cybersecurity concepts, understanding relevant tools and technologies, and practicing hands-on exercises. Demonstrating your ability to solve real-world problems is key to succeeding in technical interviews.

The Transition from Internship to Entry-Level Positions

1. Building a Strong Professional Reputation:

During internships, focus on building a strong professional reputation within the organization. Demonstrate a proactive attitude, eagerness to learn, and a strong work ethic. A positive reputation as an intern can significantly impact your chances of being considered for entry-level positions within the same organization or through referrals.

2. Seeking Feedback and Continuous Improvement:

Actively seek feedback during internships to identify areas for improvement. Use feedback as a tool for continuous learning and skill enhancement. Demonstrating a commitment to growth and improvement not only benefits your current role but also positions you as a desirable candidate for entry-level positions where a growth mindset is highly valued.

3. Networking Within the Organization:

Leverage the opportunity to network within the organization where you are interning. Attend internal cybersecurity events, engage with different teams, and seek mentorship from experienced professionals. Networking within the organization increases your visibility and may lead to internal referrals or recommendations for entry-level positions.

4. Showcasing Internship Achievements on Resumes:

When transitioning from internships to entry-level positions, strategically showcase your internship achievements on your resume. Highlight specific projects, contributions, and outcomes that demonstrate your impact. Emphasize how your practical experience during the internship has prepared you for the challenges of an entry-level cybersecurity role.

Conclusion: Launching Your Cybersecurity Career Through Practical Experience

In conclusion, gaining practical experience through internships and entry-level positions is a strategic and indispensable phase in launching a successful cybersecurity career. The hands-on learning, exposure to diverse environments, and development of critical skills during internships set the foundation for a fulfilling and impactful career in cybersecurity. Approaching internships strategically, building a strong professional reputation, and seamlessly transitioning to entry-level positions contribute to a seamless and successful career trajectory. As you embark on your journey to gain practical experience, let it be a transformative phase that propels you into the exciting and ever-evolving world of cybersecurity. May your internship experiences be rich with learning, mentorship, and practical challenges, positioning you as a dynamic and sought-after professional in the field.

Resume Building

In the dynamic field of cybersecurity, where the landscape evolves rapidly, gaining practical experience through internships and entry-level positions is instrumental in launching a successful career. As a cybersecurity professional with years of experience, I understand the strategic significance of building a robust resume. This section delves into the art of resume building specifically within the context of internships and entry-level positions, providing insights into crafting a compelling document that showcases your skills, experiences, and potential.

The Role of a Strong Resume in Cybersecurity

1. First Impression and Professional Branding:

Your resume is often the first impression you make on potential employers or recruiters. In the competitive field of cybersecurity, where the demand for skilled professionals is high, a strong resume serves as a powerful tool for creating a positive and lasting impression. It acts as a snapshot of your professional journey, highlighting key achievements, skills, and experiences.

2. Demonstrating Relevant Skills and Qualifications:

A well-crafted resume effectively communicates your relevant skills and qualifications. For individuals seeking internships or entry-level positions in cybersecurity, it is essential to align your resume with the specific requirements of the role. This includes showcasing technical skills, certifications, and academic achievements that demonstrate your readiness to contribute to cybersecurity initiatives.

3. Highlighting Practical Experience and Projects:

Internships and entry-level positions provide opportunities to gain practical experience and work on projects that showcase your abilities. Your resume should effectively highlight these experiences, detailing the projects you contributed to and the impact of your work.

This not only demonstrates your hands-on skills but also provides tangible evidence of your ability to apply theoretical knowledge in real-world scenarios.

4. Tailoring the Resume for Each Opportunity:

One of the key strategies in resume building is tailoring the document for each specific opportunity. Cybersecurity roles vary widely, encompassing areas such as penetration testing, incident response, security analysis, and more. Customize your resume to emphasize the skills and experiences most relevant to the internship or entry-level position you are applying for. This targeted approach increases your chances of standing out to recruiters.

Essential Elements of a Cybersecurity Resume

1. Clear and Concise Objective Statement:

Start your resume with a clear and concise objective statement. This brief section should articulate your career goals and convey your enthusiasm for the specific internship or entry-level position. Make it evident why you are passionate about cybersecurity and how you intend to contribute to the organization's security objectives.

2. Educational Background and Certifications:

Provide a detailed overview of your educational background, including relevant degrees and certifications. For individuals seeking entry-level positions, academic achievements are particularly important. Highlight any cybersecurity-related coursework, projects, or research that demonstrates your commitment to the field. Include certifications such as CompTIA Security+, Certified Information Systems Security Professional (CISSP), or Offensive Security Certified Professional (OSCP) if applicable.

3. Technical Skills Proficiency:

Create a dedicated section that outlines your technical skills proficiency. This is where you can showcase your expertise in programming languages, cybersecurity tools, operating systems, and other relevant technologies. Be specific and use keywords that align with the requirements of the internship or entry-level position. This section serves as a quick reference for recruiters looking for specific technical qualifications.

4. Relevant Work Experience and Internships:

The heart of your resume lies in the section detailing your work experience and internships. For each position, provide a brief description of the organization, your role, and the duration of your engagement. Focus on quantifiable achievements and the impact of your contributions. Use action verbs to convey your responsibilities and emphasize how your work added value to the organization.

5. Projects and Practical Experience:

Dedicate a section to highlight specific projects and practical experiences relevant to cybersecurity. Describe the objectives of each project, the technologies utilized, and the outcomes achieved. Whether it's a capstone project from your academic studies or a hands-on task during an internship, articulate how your involvement demonstrated your ability to address real-world cybersecurity challenges.

6. Leadership and Extracurricular Activities:

Showcase any leadership roles or involvement in extracurricular activities related to cybersecurity. This could include participation in cybersecurity clubs, organizing security-related events, or contributing to open-source projects. Leadership and extracurricular activities demonstrate your commitment to continuous learning and community engagement.

7. Soft Skills and Interpersonal Abilities:

While technical skills are paramount in cybersecurity, soft skills and interpersonal abilities are equally crucial. Include a section that highlights skills such as communication, problem-solving, teamwork, and adaptability. These qualities contribute to your overall effectiveness in collaborative cybersecurity environments.

Strategic Tips for Crafting an Impactful Cybersecurity Resume

1. Quantify Achievements and Impact:

Whenever possible, quantify your achievements and the impact of your work. For instance, mention the percentage improvement in security posture due to a specific project, or the number of vulnerabilities identified and remediated. Quantifying achievements adds a layer of credibility and conveys the tangible results of your efforts.

2. Use Action Verbs and Power Words:

Employ action verbs and power words to convey a sense of initiative and accomplishment. Instead of using generic phrases, opt for strong verbs that vividly describe your responsibilities and contributions. For example, use words like "implemented," "optimized," or "led" to enhance the impact of your statements.

3. Tailor the Resume for Each Application:

Customize your resume for each internship or entry-level position application. Analyse the specific requirements and skills sought by the employer and ensure that your resume highlights the most relevant qualifications. Tailoring your resume demonstrates a genuine interest in the role and increases your chances of being noticed by recruiters.

4. Incorporate Keywords and Phrases:

Many organizations use applicant tracking systems (ATS) to screen resumes based on keywords. To ensure your resume passes through these systems successfully, incorporate relevant keywords and phrases from the job description. Use terms specific to cybersecurity tools, technologies, and skills to align with the employer's expectations.

5. Create an Online Presence:

In addition to a traditional resume, create and maintain an online presence that complements your professional brand. Develop a LinkedIn profile highlighting your cybersecurity experience, skills, and achievements. Share articles, insights, and participate in relevant discussions within the cybersecurity community to further establish your credibility.

Conclusion: Crafting Your Cybersecurity Narrative

In conclusion, crafting a compelling resume is an integral aspect of building your cybersecurity career, especially when seeking internships and entry-level positions. Your resume serves as your professional narrative, showcasing your skills, experiences, and potential contributions to prospective employers. By strategically presenting your educational background, technical skills, work experience, and projects, you create a document that not only highlights your capabilities but also aligns with the unique requirements of the cybersecurity roles you are pursuing. Approach resume building as an ongoing process, refining and tailoring your document for each opportunity. May your cybersecurity resume be a testament to your passion for the field, your commitment to excellence, and your readiness to contribute to the ever-evolving landscape of cybersecurity.

Navigating the Job Market

In the dynamic and rapidly evolving landscape of cybersecurity, securing internships and entry-level positions is a critical step in gaining practical experience and launching a successful career. Navigating the job market in cybersecurity requires a strategic approach, given the diverse opportunities, specialized roles, and evolving industry demands. As an experienced cybersecurity professional, I share insights on effectively navigating the job market to secure internships and entry-level positions.

Understanding the Cybersecurity Job Market

1. Diversity of Roles and Specializations:

The cybersecurity job market is characterized by a rich diversity of roles and specializations. From penetration testers and incident responders to security analysts and engineers, there are numerous paths to explore. Understanding the nuances of these roles is essential when navigating the job market, as it enables you to align your skills and interests with the right opportunities.

2. Evolving Skill Requirements:

The skill requirements in cybersecurity are continually evolving, driven by technological advancements and emerging threat landscapes. Employers seek candidates with a blend of technical expertise, hands-on experience, and soft skills. Keeping abreast of the latest trends and aligning your skill set with industry demands positions you as a competitive candidate in the job market.

3. Industry-Specific Certifications:

Certifications play a pivotal role in the cybersecurity job market. Employers often look for candidates with industry-recognized certifications that validate their skills and knowledge. Certifications such as CompTIA Security+, Certified Information Systems Security Professional (CISSP), and Offensive Security Certified Professional (OSCP) are highly regarded. Tailoring your certification portfolio to the specific roles you're interested in enhances your marketability.

4. Networking and Community Engagement:

Networking is a powerful strategy for navigating the cybersecurity job market. Engaging with the cybersecurity community through events, conferences, online forums, and social media platforms allows you to connect with professionals, recruiters, and potential employers. Building a strong professional network not only provides insights into job opportunities but can also lead to referrals and recommendations.

Strategic Approaches to Navigating the Job Market

1. Define Your Career Goals:

Before diving into the job market, take the time to define your career goals within cybersecurity. Identify the specific roles or specializations that align with your interests and skills. Understanding your career goals enables you to target relevant opportunities and tailor your job searches accordingly.

2. Conduct Thorough Research:

Research is a key component of navigating the job market successfully. Explore different organizations, industries, and sectors to identify those aligned with your career goals. Investigate their cybersecurity programs, initiatives, and the types of roles they offer. Tailoring your applications to organizations that resonate with your goals increases your chances of finding the right fit.

3. Build a Strong Online Presence:

Establishing a strong online presence is crucial in the digital age. Create a professional LinkedIn profile that showcases your skills, experiences, and achievements. Actively participate in relevant discussions, share insights, and connect with professionals in the cybersecurity field. A well-crafted online presence serves as an extension of your resume and enhances your visibility in the job market.

4. Utilize Job Search Platforms:

Leverage job search platforms and websites dedicated to cybersecurity positions. Platforms like CyberSecJobs, InfoSec Jobs, and specialized sections on general job boards provide a curated list of cybersecurity opportunities. Use advanced search features to filter positions based on your preferred location, role, and skill requirements.

Crafting a Standout Resume for Cybersecurity Positions

1. Tailor Your Resume for Each Application:

A generic resume may not effectively convey your suitability for specific cybersecurity roles. Tailor your resume for each application by aligning it with the specific requirements of the position. Highlight relevant skills, experiences, and certifications that directly correlate with the job description. This targeted approach increases your chances of capturing the attention of recruiters.

2. Showcase Your Practical Experience:

Internships and entry-level positions often emphasize practical experience. Showcase your hands-on experience in cybersecurity through internships, academic projects, or personal initiatives. Highlight specific projects, tools, and technologies you've worked with, and quantify your impact wherever possible. A resume rich in practical experiences demonstrates your readiness to contribute from day one.

3. Emphasize Certifications and Training:

Certifications are valuable assets in the cybersecurity job market. Emphasize relevant certifications and training programs on your resume to showcase your commitment to continuous learning. Include details such as certification names, issuing bodies, and dates of attainment. Certifications act as tangible validations of your skills and can serve as key differentiators.

4. Highlight Technical and Soft Skills:

Clearly highlight both technical and soft skills on your resume. Technical skills demonstrate your proficiency in key cybersecurity tools, programming languages, and technologies. Soft skills, such as communication, problem-solving, and teamwork, are equally important in collaborative cybersecurity environments. Striking a balance between technical and soft skills enhances your overall suitability for the role.

Strategies for Securing Internships and Entry-Level Positions

1. Apply for Internships Strategically:

Internships are valuable opportunities to gain practical experience and make meaningful contributions to cybersecurity initiatives. Apply for internships strategically by targeting organizations aligned with your interests and career goals. Research internship programs offered by cybersecurity firms, government agencies, and corporate entities to find the best fit.

2. Participate in Cybersecurity Competitions:

Engaging in cybersecurity competitions is an excellent way to showcase your skills and gain visibility in the job market. Participate in Capture The Flag (CTF) competitions, hackathons, and challenges that allow you to demonstrate your problem-solving abilities. Winning or performing well in these competitions can attract the attention of recruiters looking for talented individuals.

3. Seek Mentorship and Guidance:

Mentorship plays a crucial role in career development. Seek mentorship from experienced cybersecurity professionals who can provide guidance on navigating the job market, refining your resume, and preparing for interviews. Mentors can share insights based on their own experiences and help you navigate the complexities of the cybersecurity field.

4. Stay Informed and Adapt:

The cybersecurity landscape is dynamic, with new technologies and threats emerging regularly. Stay informed about industry trends, advancements, and best practices. Adapt your skill set based on the evolving demands of the job market. Continuous learning and adaptability are highly valued in cybersecurity professionals.

Conclusion: Charting Your Path in Cybersecurity

In conclusion, navigating the job market for internships and entry-level positions in cybersecurity requires a combination of strategic planning, targeted applications, and a commitment to continuous learning. Understanding the diverse roles within the field, staying informed about industry trends, and building a strong online presence contribute to your success in securing meaningful opportunities. Craft a standout resume that showcases your practical experiences, technical skills, and certifications, and utilize strategic approaches such as networking and mentorship to enhance your visibility in the cybersecurity community. As you embark on your journey to gain practical experience, remember that each step is a valuable investment in your cybersecurity career. May your efforts lead to meaningful internships, entry-level positions, and a trajectory that aligns with your aspirations in the dynamic and impactful field of cybersecurity.

Open-Source Contributions and GitHub Presence

Joining Cybersecurity Communities

In the ever-evolving landscape of cybersecurity, gaining practical experience is essential for launching a successful career. This chapter delves into the strategic importance of open-source contributions, cultivating a meaningful GitHub presence, and actively participating in cybersecurity communities. As an experienced cybersecurity professional, I understand the transformative power of collaboration and community engagement in shaping a robust cybersecurity career.

The Significance of Open-Source Contributions

1. Collaborative Learning and Skill Enhancement:

Open-source projects serve as dynamic platforms for collaborative learning and skill enhancement. Contributing to projects exposes individuals to diverse perspectives, coding styles, and problem-solving approaches. For aspiring cybersecurity professionals, active involvement in open source provides hands-on experience with real-world challenges, fostering a deep understanding of cybersecurity concepts.

2. Building a Portfolio of Practical Achievements:

Open-source contributions contribute to building a portfolio of practical achievements. Aspiring professionals can showcase their ability to collaborate on meaningful projects, contribute to codebases, and address security issues. A strong portfolio, hosted on platforms like GitHub, becomes a tangible representation of your skills and commitment to the cybersecurity community.

3. Exposure to Industry-Standard Tools and Practices:

Many open-source projects align with industry-standard tools and practices. By actively contributing to such projects, individuals gain exposure to the tools, methodologies, and coding standards prevalent in the cybersecurity field. This exposure is invaluable for honing technical skills and staying current with industry trends.

4. Establishing a Reputation in the Community:

Open-source contributions enable individuals to establish a reputation within the broader cybersecurity community. Recognition for meaningful contributions, code reviews, and collaborative efforts enhances your visibility as a capable and engaged cybersecurity professional. A positive reputation is an asset when seeking internships, entry-level positions, or networking opportunities.

Strategic Approaches to Joining Cybersecurity Communities

1. Identifying Relevant Communities:

The cybersecurity landscape is rich with diverse communities catering to various specializations. Identify communities aligned with your interests and career goals. Whether focused on penetration testing, threat intelligence, or secure coding practices, find communities that resonate with your aspirations. Popular platforms include forums, social media groups, and dedicated community websites.

2. Active Participation in Discussions:

Actively participate in discussions within cybersecurity communities. Share your insights, ask questions, and contribute to conversations. Engaging with experienced professionals and fellow enthusiasts not only expands your knowledge but also establishes you as an active and collaborative member of the community. Meaningful interactions can lead to mentorship opportunities and valuable connections.

3. Contribution to Knowledge Sharing:

Contribute to knowledge sharing within cybersecurity communities by sharing articles, tutorials, and insights. Establishing yourself as a resourceful contributor enhances your reputation and positions you as someone committed to the community's growth. Platforms like blogs, podcasts, or even hosting webinars can be avenues for sharing your expertise.

4. Collaborating on Open-Source Projects:

Actively seek and collaborate on open-source projects relevant to cybersecurity. Platforms like GitHub host a myriad of projects spanning different aspects of cybersecurity, from tools and frameworks to threat intelligence platforms. Contributing to open source projects not only enhances your technical skills but also provides a tangible record of your contributions for potential employers to see.

Building and Showcasing Your GitHub Presence

1. Optimizing Your GitHub Profile:

Your GitHub profile serves as a digital resume for potential employers and community members. Optimize your profile by providing a clear and concise bio that highlights your cybersecurity interests and expertise. Include links to personal websites, blogs, or portfolios that complement your GitHub presence.

2. Creating a Repository for Your Work:

Create a dedicated repository to showcase your cybersecurity-related work. This could include scripts, tools, or write-ups from challenges and projects. Use a README file to provide context, instructions, and documentation for your contributions. A well-curated repository demonstrates your skills, projects, and commitment to open-source collaboration.

3. Highlighting Contributions and Achievements:

Use GitHub's features to highlight your contributions and achievements. Pin significant repositories or projects to your profile to showcase them prominently. Utilize the "Contribution Graph" to demonstrate your consistency and activity. Ensure that your commit messages are clear and informative, detailing the purpose and impact of your contributions.

4. Engaging in Code Reviews and Collaboration:

Actively engage in code reviews and collaborative efforts on GitHub. Providing constructive feedback on others' work demonstrates your understanding of cybersecurity best practices and your commitment to maintaining code quality. Collaborating with peers on GitHub projects allows you to leverage collective expertise and refine your own skills.

Strategies for Leveraging Open Source for Career Advancement

1. Networking Opportunities:

Open-source contributions open doors to networking opportunities within the cybersecurity community. Engage with maintainers, contributors, and community leaders. Attend virtual meetups, conferences, and events organized by the communities you're involved in. Networking within open-source projects can lead to mentorship, collaborative projects, and potential job referrals.

2. Skill Development and Continuous Learning:

Actively contributing to open-source projects facilitates continuous skill development and learning. The collaborative nature of open source encourages exposure to new technologies, coding practices, and security challenges. Embrace the learning opportunities embedded in open-source projects to stay agile and relevant in the ever-evolving cybersecurity landscape.

3. Showcasing Expertise to Employers:

Your GitHub presence becomes a powerful tool for showcasing your expertise to potential employers. When seeking internships or entry-level positions, recruiters often review GitHub profiles to gauge practical skills and contributions. Ensure that your GitHub repositories align with the skills and technologies relevant to the positions you are interested in.

4. Contributing to Security Research:

Open-source communities often play a role in advancing security research. Contribute to security-related research projects, share your findings, and collaborate with researchers in the community. Involvement in such projects not only enhances your credibility but also positions you at the forefront of emerging trends and innovations in cybersecurity.

Conclusion: Empowering Your Cybersecurity Journey

In conclusion, actively participating in open-source communities and cultivating a meaningful GitHub presence are strategic pillars in gaining practical experience and advancing your cybersecurity career. Open-source contributions provide avenues for collaborative learning, skill enhancement, and establishing a reputable presence within the cybersecurity community. By joining relevant communities, actively participating in discussions, and contributing to open-source projects, you empower your cybersecurity journey with practical experiences, networking opportunities, and a dynamic showcase of your skills. As you embark on this strategic path, may your open-source endeavours become a catalyst for continuous growth, community impact, and career advancement in the dynamic and ever-evolving field of cybersecurity.

Contributing to Open-Source Projects

In the dynamic realm of cybersecurity, gaining practical experience is a cornerstone for launching a successful career. This chapter focuses on the strategic significance of contributing to open-source projects and building a robust GitHub presence. As an experienced cybersecurity professional, I recognize the transformative impact of active participation in the open-source community on skill development, networking, and career advancement.

The Power of Contributing to Open-Source Projects

1. Hands-On Learning in Real-World Scenarios:

Contributing to open-source projects provides unparalleled hands-on learning experiences in real-world scenarios. Cybersecurity is a field where theoretical knowledge is most effectively complemented by practical application. By engaging with open-source projects, aspiring professionals gain exposure to actual challenges faced by the community, honing their problem-solving skills and deepening their understanding of cybersecurity concepts.

2. Collaboration and Teamwork:

Open-source projects are collaborative endeavours that bring together diverse skill sets, experiences, and perspectives. Contributing to these projects fosters a culture of collaboration and teamwork, which are critical skills in the cybersecurity industry. Understanding how to work effectively within a team, even in a virtual environment, is an asset that goes beyond technical proficiency.

3. Exposure to Cutting-Edge Technologies:

The open-source community is often at the forefront of technological innovations. Contributing to projects exposes individuals to cutting-edge technologies, tools, and frameworks used in cybersecurity. This exposure is invaluable for staying abreast of industry trends, understanding emerging threats, and adapting to the rapidly evolving cybersecurity landscape.

4. Building a Professional Network:

The open-source community serves as a vast networking platform where professionals, enthusiasts, and experts converge. Contributing to projects allows individuals to build a professional network by interacting with maintainers, collaborators, and fellow contributors. Networking within the open-source community can lead to mentorship opportunities, knowledge sharing, and even potential job referrals.

Strategic Approaches to Contributing to Open-Source Projects

1. Identifying Projects Aligned with Interests:

The first step in contributing to open-source projects is identifying those aligned with your cybersecurity interests. Whether your passion lies in penetration testing, cryptography, or threat intelligence, there are open-source projects covering a broad spectrum of cybersecurity domains. Platforms like GitHub provide filters and search functionalities to help you discover projects matching your expertise and aspirations.

2. Understanding Project Contributions Guidelines:

Each open-source project has its unique set of contribution guidelines. Before diving in, thoroughly understand the guidelines provided by the project maintainers. This includes the preferred communication channels, coding standards, documentation requirements, and the process for submitting contributions. Adhering to these guidelines ensures a smooth integration of your contributions into the project.

3. Starting with Small Contributions:

For individuals new to open-source contributions, starting with small, manageable tasks is advisable. This could include fixing documentation errors, addressing minor bugs, or contributing to ongoing discussions. Small contributions allow you to familiarize yourself with the project's codebase, development processes, and the dynamics of collaborative work.

4. Engaging in Code Reviews:

Actively engaging in code reviews is a valuable contribution to open-source projects. Reviewing others' code not only enhances your understanding of different coding styles and practices but also allows you to provide constructive feedback. Engaging in code reviews is a collaborative process that strengthens your relationship with the project community and demonstrates your commitment to improving code quality.

Showcasing Your Open-Source Contributions on GitHub

1. Creating an Impactful GitHub Profile:

Your GitHub profile is a digital representation of your skills, contributions, and involvement in the open-source community. Ensure that your profile is impactful by featuring a clear and concise bio, a professional profile picture, and relevant contact information. The overall presentation of your GitHub profile should reflect your commitment to cybersecurity and open source collaboration.

2. Showcasing Projects on Your Profile:

Use GitHub's repository features to showcase your contributions and personal projects. Pinning significant repositories to your profile ensures They are prominently displayed. Include a diverse range of projects, emphasizing your expertise in different cybersecurity areas. Each project should have a well-crafted README file that provides context, instructions, and documentation for potential collaborators or employers.

3. Highlighting Contributions in the Contribution Graph:

GitHub's Contribution Graph visually represents your activity and contributions over time. Ensure that your contribution graph reflects consistency and engagement. Regular contributions, even if they are small, demonstrate your ongoing commitment to the open source community. A vibrant contribution graph is a positive indicator of your involvement in collaborative projects.

4. Creating a Portfolio Repository:

Consider creating a dedicated repository on GitHub to serve as a portfolio of your open-source contributions. This repository can include links to relevant projects, summaries of your contributions, and documentation showcasing your growth and expertise. A well-curated portfolio repository becomes a central reference for potential employers or collaborators to assess your skills and contributions.

Strategies for Maximizing the Impact of Your Contributions

1. Demonstrating Consistency:

Consistency is key when contributing to open source projects. Regularly engage with the community, make meaningful contributions, and maintain an active presence on relevant platforms. Demonstrating consistency showcases your dedication to continuous learning and collaboration, traits highly valued in the cybersecurity industry.

2. Showcasing Problem-Solving Skills:

Cybersecurity professionals are often tasked with solving complex problems. Use your contributions to open source projects as opportunities to showcase your problem-solving skills. Addressing issues, proposing innovative solutions, and actively participating in discussions demonstrate your analytical mindset and ability to navigate challenges effectively.

3. Collaborating Across Disciplines:

Cybersecurity is a multidisciplinary field that intersects with various domains, including software development, networking, and cryptography. Actively seek opportunities to collaborate across these disciplines within open source projects. Engaging in cross-functional collaboration not only expands your skill set but also positions you as a versatile professional capable of navigating diverse cybersecurity challenges.

4. Seeking Feedback and Iterating:

Embrace feedback as an essential part of the open source contribution process. Seek feedback from project maintainers, peers, and community members. Use constructive criticism to iterate on your contributions and enhance the quality of your work. The ability to receive and incorporate feedback is a valuable skill that contributes to your growth as a cybersecurity professional.

Conclusion: Charting Your Course in Open-Source Collaboration

In conclusion, contributing to open-source projects is a strategic pathway to gaining practical experience and establishing a robust presence in the cybersecurity community. The hands-on learning, collaborative opportunities, and networking potential within the open-source realm are unparalleled. By identifying projects aligned with your interests, understanding contribution guidelines, and actively engaging in code reviews, you position yourself as a valuable contributor in the dynamic and ever-evolving field of cybersecurity.

Showcasing your open-source contributions on GitHub becomes a powerful tool for showcasing your skills and commitment to potential employers. A well-curated GitHub profile, featuring impactful projects, contributions, and a vibrant contribution graph, enhances your visibility within the cybersecurity community. As you embark on your journey of open-source collaboration, may your contributions be a testament to your passion for cybersecurity, your dedication to continuous learning, and your readiness to make a meaningful impact in the cybersecurity landscape.

Chapter 8: Networking and Mentoring

Building a Professional Network

LinkedIn and Social Media Presence

In the dynamic and interconnected field of cybersecurity, building a professional network is a strategic imperative for career growth and advancement. This chapter explores the nuances of creating a robust network, with a specific focus on leveraging platforms like LinkedIn and other social media channels. As an experienced cybersecurity professional, I understand the transformative power of networking in shaping a successful and fulfilling career.

The Importance of Building a Professional Network in Cybersecurity

1. Opportunities for Collaboration and Knowledge Sharing:

A professional network in cybersecurity opens doors to opportunities for collaboration and knowledge sharing. The field thrives on collective intelligence, and networking allows you to tap into a wealth of experiences and insights. Engaging with professionals from diverse backgrounds, roles, and industries fosters a rich exchange of ideas, best practices, and lessons learned.

2. Access to Job Opportunities:

Networking is a powerful avenue for discovering job opportunities within the cybersecurity landscape. Many positions are filled through referrals and recommendations. Building a network of industry professionals increases your visibility and the likelihood of being informed about relevant job openings. It also positions you as a candidate recommended by trusted connections, enhancing your credibility in the job market.

3. Stay Informed About Industry Trends:

The cybersecurity landscape is dynamic, with new threats, technologies, and best practices emerging regularly. A well-established professional network serves as a reliable source for staying informed about industry trends. Engaging with professionals on platforms like LinkedIn allows you to access and share the latest insights, research findings, and news within the cybersecurity community.

4. Mentorship and Guidance:

A strong professional network provides opportunities for mentorship and guidance, which are invaluable assets in career development. Connecting with experienced professionals who have navigated similar career paths allows you to benefit from their insights, advice, and wisdom. Mentorship relationships can provide direction, encouragement, and a roadmap for overcoming challenges in your cybersecurity journey.

Strategic Approaches to Building a Professional Network on LinkedIn and Social Media

1. Optimizing Your LinkedIn Profile:

LinkedIn stands out as a leading platform for professional networking, particularly in the cybersecurity industry. Begin by optimizing your LinkedIn profile to make a strong first impression. Ensure that your profile photo is professional, your headline reflects your current role or aspirations, and your summary provides a compelling overview of your cybersecurity expertise, interests, and career goals.

2. Tailoring Connection Requests:

When sending connection requests on LinkedIn, tailor each request to make it personalized and meaningful. Clearly express why you want to connect, highlighting shared interests, mutual connections, or common professional goals. A personalized connection request is more likely to be accepted, and it sets the stage for meaningful interactions.

3. Participating in LinkedIn Groups:

Joining and actively participating in cybersecurity-related LinkedIn groups is an effective way to expand your network. These groups provide forums for discussions, knowledge sharing, and networking with professionals who share similar interests. Engage in conversations, ask questions, and contribute insights to establish your presence within these communities.

4. Publishing Thoughtful Content:

Elevate your LinkedIn and social media presence by publishing thoughtful and relevant content. Share articles, insights, and your own perspectives on cybersecurity trends, challenges, and solutions. Regularly contributing to the industry conversation positions you as a thought leader and attracts professionals interested in engaging with valuable content.

Leveraging Social Media Beyond LinkedIn

1. Twitter for Real-Time Updates:

Twitter is a dynamic platform known for real-time updates and conversations. Follow cybersecurity experts, organizations, and industry influencers to stay informed about the latest news, events, and discussions. Engage with tweets, retweet relevant content, and use hashtags to connect with the broader cybersecurity community.

2. Professional Branding on Instagram:

While Instagram is often associated with visual content, it can also be a platform for professional branding in cybersecurity. Share snapshots of your work environment, conferences, or cybersecurity-themed visuals. Craft a professional and approachable image that aligns with your career goals and showcases your passion for the field.

3. Engaging with Cybersecurity Communities on Reddit:

Reddit hosts various cybersecurity communities, known as subreddits, where professionals and enthusiasts discuss a wide range of topics. Actively participating in these communities allows you to connect with like-minded individuals, seek advice, and contribute to discussions. Reddit provides a unique and informal platform for networking within the cybersecurity community.

4. Connecting on Professional Platforms like Xing:

Explore professional platforms beyond the mainstream, such as Xing, which is particularly popular in certain regions. Building a presence on platforms that cater to specific professional communities can broaden your reach and connect you with professionals who might not be as active on more global platforms.

Strategies for Effective Networking in Cybersecurity

1. Strategic Relationship Building:

Approach networking strategically by identifying professionals who align with your career goals or possess expertise you admire. Focus on building meaningful relationships rather than aiming for quantity. Engage in conversations, express genuine interest, and be proactive in nurturing connections over time.

2. Networking at Conferences and Events:

Attend cybersecurity conferences, workshops, and events to network with professionals in person. Conferences offer unparalleled opportunities to meet industry leaders, experts, and potential mentors. Actively participate in networking sessions, join discussions, and exchange contact information to extend your professional network beyond the digital realm.

3. Initiating Informational Interviews:

Informational interviews are valuable tools for networking and gaining insights into specific roles or organizations. Reach out to professionals for informational interviews to learn about their career paths, industry experiences, and advice. These interviews not only expand your network but also provide valuable guidance in shaping your cybersecurity career.

4. Contributing to Open-Source Projects:

As discussed in the previous chapter, contributing to open-source projects is not only a hands-on learning experience but also a powerful networking strategy. Engage with project maintainers, fellow contributors, and the broader community. Your active involvement in open-source projects can lead to meaningful connections, mentorship opportunities, and potential collaborations.

Maintaining and Nurturing Your Professional Network

1. Regular Engagement on Social Media:

Consistent engagement on social media is crucial for maintaining and nurturing your professional network. Regularly share updates, congratulate connections on their achievements, and engage in discussions. Being actively present on these platforms reinforces your commitment to the cybersecurity community.

2. Periodic Check-Ins with Connections:

Periodically check in with your connections through personalized messages. Inquire about their professional endeavours, share relevant content, or seek their opinion on industry trends. These periodic check-ins go beyond virtual connections, demonstrating genuine interest in fostering relationships.

3. Participating in Virtual Events and Webinars:

In the era of virtual connectivity, participate in webinars, virtual events, and online meetups. These platforms provide opportunities to expand your network, connect with professionals worldwide, and engage in discussions on the latest trends and challenges in cybersecurity.

4. Giving Back Through Mentorship:

As you progress in your cybersecurity career, consider giving back to the community through mentorship. Mentorship is a two-way street, and sharing your experiences, insights, and knowledge with less experienced professionals not only contributes to the community but also strengthens your position as a respected and influential figure in the field.

Conclusion: Navigating the Networked Landscape of Cybersecurity

In conclusion, building a professional network is an integral aspect of navigating the dynamic landscape of cybersecurity. Leveraging platforms like LinkedIn and other social media channels enhances your visibility, opens doors to opportunities, and provides a platform for ongoing learning and collaboration. Whether you are connecting with professionals on LinkedIn, engaging in discussions on Twitter, or participating in cybersecurity communities on Reddit, the strategic cultivation of your network is a powerful asset in shaping a successful and fulfilling cybersecurity career.

As you embark on your networking journey, remember that the strength of your network lies not only in its size but in the quality of connections and the depth of relationships you build. Nurturing your professional network requires ongoing effort, genuine engagement, and a commitment to lifelong learning and collaboration. May your network serve as a catalyst for continuous growth, meaningful connections, and impactful contributions in the vibrant and interconnected world of cybersecurity.

Building a Professional Network

Attending Conferences and Meetups

In the ever-evolving landscape of cybersecurity, building a robust professional network is a strategic imperative for aspiring professionals. This chapter explores the significance of attending conferences and meetups as a targeted approach to expanding your network within the cybersecurity community. As an experienced cybersecurity professional, I recognize the transformative power of in-person interactions in shaping a successful and fulfilling career.

The Power of In-Person Networking in Cybersecurity

1. Face-to-Face Connections:

While virtual interactions have become more prevalent, the value of face-to-face connections cannot be overstated. Conferences and meetups provide a unique environment for professionals to engage in meaningful conversations, share experiences, and establish a personal connection. In the dynamic field of cybersecurity, these personal connections can be instrumental in fostering collaborations and opening doors to new opportunities.

2. Exposure to Diverse Perspectives:

Cybersecurity conferences and meetups attract professionals from various backgrounds, industries, and specializations. Attending such events exposes you to diverse perspectives, challenges, and solutions within the cybersecurity domain. The richness of these interactions contributes to your professional growth by broadening your understanding of the field and providing insights into different facets of cybersecurity.

3. Access to Industry Leaders and Experts:

One of the key advantages of attending conferences is the opportunity to interact with industry leaders and experts. These events often feature keynote speakers, panel discussions, and workshops led by seasoned professionals. Engaging with these thought leaders allows you to gain insights into the latest trends, emerging technologies, and best practices in cybersecurity directly from those who shape the industry.

4. Networking Beyond Digital Boundaries:

While digital platforms facilitate networking, conferences and meetups offer a tangible and immersive networking experience. The casual interactions during coffee breaks, networking sessions, and social events create a conducive environment for building relationships beyond the constraints of virtual communication. These real-world connections often translate into lasting professional collaborations.

Strategic Approaches to Maximizing Conference and Meetup Networking

1. Research and Selective Participation

Before attending a conference or meetup, conduct thorough research on the event's agenda, speakers, and participants. Choose events that align with your cybersecurity interests and career goals. Some conferences may focus on specific areas like threat intelligence, while others cover a broader spectrum of cybersecurity topics. Selective participation ensures that your time and resources are invested in events most relevant to your professional aspirations.

2. Prepare an Elevator Pitch:

A well-crafted elevator pitch is an essential tool for making a strong impression during networking events. Clearly articulate who you are, your areas of expertise or interest in cybersecurity, and your career objectives. An effective elevator pitch not only introduces you concisely but also sparks interest and facilitates meaningful conversations with fellow professionals.

3. Active Participation in Discussions:

Conferences often include panel discussions, Q&A sessions, and interactive workshops. Actively participate in these discussions to showcase your knowledge, ask insightful questions, and engage with speakers and fellow attendees. Your active involvement positions you as a proactive and engaged member of the cybersecurity community, enhancing your visibility and networking opportunities.

4. Utilize Networking Platforms:

Many conferences and meetups provide dedicated networking platforms or mobile apps. These platforms allow participants to connect, schedule meetings, and exchange contact information. Leverage these tools to expand your network during the event. Reach out to professionals with shared interests, express your desire to connect, and schedule follow-up discussions to continue the conversation.

Strategies for Maximizing the Impact of Conference and Meetup Networking

1. Attend Industry-Relevant Events:

Identify and prioritize industry-relevant events that align with your cybersecurity specialization or career goals. If you are interested in ethical hacking, for example, attending conferences like DEF CON or Black Hat may provide specific insights and networking opportunities within that niche. Tailoring your attendance to events directly related to your interests ensures a targeted and impactful experience.

2. Engage in Post-Event Follow-Up:

The impact of networking at conferences extends beyond the event itself. After attending a conference or meetup, engage in post-event follow-up activities. Connect with professionals you met on LinkedIn, express gratitude for insightful conversations, and share any relevant resources or insights. Building on the connections made during the event contributes to the longevity and depth of your professional network.

3. Participate in Networking Dinners and Social Events:

Many conferences and meetups include networking dinners, social events, or informal gatherings. Attend these activities to connect with professionals in a more relaxed setting. Informal interactions outside the structured conference environment often lead to deeper connections and provide opportunities for more extended discussions on shared interests or potential collaborations.

4. Contribute as a Speaker or Panelist:

As your expertise grows, consider contributing to conferences and meetups as a speaker or panelist. Sharing your knowledge and experiences not only positions you as an industry expert but also provides a unique platform for networking. Attendees often seek out speakers for further discussions, creating opportunities for meaningful connections and collaborations.

Navigating Networking Challenges at Conferences and Meetups

1. Overcoming Introversion:

Networking can be challenging, especially for individuals who identify as introverted. If you fall into this category, set realistic goals for interactions, and gradually challenge yourself to initiate conversations. Attend smaller group sessions or workshops where interactions may feel less intimidating and focus on the quality of connections rather than the quantity.

2. Dealing with Imposter Syndrome:

Imposter syndrome can affect professionals at all career stages, leading to feelings of inadequacy or self-doubt. Recognize that many attendees, including experienced professionals, may share similar sentiments. Approach networking with the mindset of continuous learning and growth and remember that everyone has unique perspectives and contributions to offer.

3. Managing Time Effectively:

Conferences often feature a packed schedule, and managing your time effectively is crucial. Prioritize key sessions, allocate time for networking breaks, and be selective in the events you attend. Quality interactions are often more valuable than a high quantity of brief encounters. Balancing your schedule allows you to make the most of both learning opportunities and networking engagements.

4. Adapting to Virtual Conferences:

In the era of remote work and virtual events, adapting to networking challenges in a digital environment is essential. Engage in virtual breakout sessions, participate in online discussions, and use virtual networking tools provided by conference platforms. While the dynamics are different from in-person events, virtual conferences still offer valuable networking opportunities that can be leveraged effectively.

Conclusion: Transformative Networking in the Cybersecurity Community

In conclusion, attending conferences and meetups is a strategic approach to building a professional network with lasting impact in the cybersecurity community. The in-person interactions, exposure to diverse perspectives, and access to industry leaders contribute significantly to your professional growth and career advancement. By adopting strategic approaches, maximizing the impact of networking, and navigating potential challenges, you can transform your networking experiences into valuable connections, collaborations, and opportunities in the dynamic and interconnected world of cybersecurity.

As you embark on your journey of conference and meetup networking, may each interaction be a steppingstone toward a thriving and resilient professional network that propels you toward continued success in your cybersecurity career.

Finding a Mentor

Mentoring Programs and Developing Mutually Beneficial Relationships

In the dynamic and fast-paced world of cybersecurity, finding a mentor can be a transformative step in one's professional journey. This chapter delves into the strategic approaches to finding a mentor, the role of mentoring programs, and the development of mutually beneficial relationships in the cybersecurity field. As an experienced cybersecurity professional, I recognize the pivotal role mentorship plays in career growth and success.

The Significance of Mentorship in Cybersecurity

1. Guidance and Career Direction:

Mentorship provides invaluable guidance and insights that are often critical in navigating the multifaceted landscape of cybersecurity. A mentor, drawing from their experiences, can offer direction, share lessons learned, and help mentees make informed decisions about their career paths.

2. Skill Development and Knowledge Transfer:

The field of cybersecurity demands a diverse skill set, and mentorship is a powerful avenue for skill development. Mentors can provide hands-on guidance, share best practices, and facilitate knowledge transfer. This practical aspect of mentorship accelerates the learning curve for mentees, enabling them to acquire skills and insights that might take years to develop independently.

3. Networking and Professional Connections:

Beyond skill development, mentors often serve as gateways to professional networks. Through mentorship, mentees gain access to a broader community of cybersecurity professionals, creating opportunities for networking, collaboration, and exposure to different facets of the industry.

4. Navigating Challenges and Building Resilience:

The cybersecurity landscape is fraught with challenges, and mentorship equips individuals with the resilience needed to overcome obstacles. Mentors, having weathered their fair share of challenges, can provide perspective, share coping mechanisms, and offer encouragement during difficult times.

Strategic Approaches to Finding a Mentor

1. Self-Assessment and Goal Clarity:

Before seeking a mentor, conduct a self-assessment to identify your strengths, weaknesses, and areas for improvement. Clearly define your career goals and aspirations within the cybersecurity field. Having a solid understanding of your own needs and objectives is a crucial foundation for finding a mentor whose expertise aligns with your goals.

2. Networking Within the Industry:

Actively participate in industry events, conferences, and online forums to expand your professional network. Networking provides opportunities to encounter potential mentors naturally. Engage in conversations, express your career interests, and seek out professionals whose experiences align with your goals. Networking platforms like LinkedIn can be particularly useful for identifying potential mentors.

3. Seeking Guidance from Peers and Colleagues:

Peer recommendations can be valuable in mentorship. Seek guidance from colleagues, peers, or industry connections who may know professionals with the expertise you are looking for. Colleagues who have benefited from mentorship themselves may be particularly insightful in recommending mentors who are supportive and effective in guiding career development.

4. Participating in Mentoring Programs:

Many organizations and industry associations offer mentoring programs as part of their commitment to professional development. Participating in such programs can provide structured mentorship opportunities. These programs often pair mentees with experienced mentors based on shared interests, creating a conducive environment for meaningful and targeted guidance.

Mentoring Programs: A Structured Path to Mentorship

1. Industry-Specific Mentorship Programs:

Industry-specific mentorship programs, often facilitated by cybersecurity organizations or professional associations, aim to connect experienced professionals with individuals seeking mentorship. These programs typically have established structures, matching criteria, and defined goals, creating a conducive environment for productive mentor-mentee relationships.

2. Academic Mentorship Initiatives:

Academic institutions with cybersecurity programs may have mentorship initiatives that connect students or recent graduates with experienced professionals in the field. These programs bridge the gap between academia and industry, providing mentees with insights into real-world applications of cybersecurity concepts.

3. Corporate Mentorship Programs:

Many corporations recognize the value of mentorship in fostering talent development and employee satisfaction. Corporate mentorship programs pair employees with mentors within the organization. These programs offer mentees insights into the organization's cybersecurity practices, career advancement opportunities, and a broader understanding of the corporate cybersecurity landscape.

4. Online Mentorship Platforms:

The digital era has seen the rise of online platforms specifically designed to connect mentors and mentees across various industries. Platforms like MentorcliQ, LinkedIn's Career Advice feature, and others facilitate virtual mentorship engagements. These platforms often provide tools for setting goals, tracking progress, and ensuring a structured and productive mentorship experience.

Developing Mutually Beneficial Relationships in Mentorship

1. Setting Clear Expectations:

Clear communication and goal-setting are fundamental to a successful mentor-mentee relationship. At the outset, articulate your expectations, goals, and areas where you seek guidance. Similarly, mentors should communicate their expectations and the level of commitment they can provide. Establishing a shared understanding lays the groundwork for a mutually beneficial partnership.

2. Regular and Structured Interactions:

Regular and structured interactions are essential for the ongoing success of the mentorship. Establish a cadence for meetings, whether it is weekly, bi-weekly, or monthly, and create a framework for discussion topics. Structured interactions provide a sense of continuity and allow both mentor and mentee to track progress and address evolving needs.

3. Active Listening and Feedback:

Mentorship is a two-way street that thrives on active listening and constructive feedback. Mentors should actively listen to their mentees' challenges, aspirations, and questions. Simultaneously, mentees should be open to feedback, suggestions, and insights provided by their mentors. A culture of open communication fosters a collaborative and supportive mentorship dynamic.

4. Mutual Learning and Growth:

Mentorship is not a one-sided process; both mentors and mentees have opportunities for learning and growth. Mentees bring fresh perspectives, innovative ideas, and the latest insights from academic or entry-level experiences. Mentors, on the other hand, contribute industry wisdom, practical guidance, and lessons learned from years of experience. Embracing the concept of mutual learning enhances the richness of the mentorship relationship.

Navigating Challenges in Mentorship

1. Addressing Mismatched Expectations:

Mismatched expectations can occur when mentors and mentees have differing views on the goals or structure of the mentorship. Addressing this challenge requires open communication to align expectations and make necessary adjustments. Regular check-ins on progress and adjustments to the mentorship plan can help prevent or address any emerging disparities.

2. Balancing Time Commitments:

Time commitments can be a challenge in mentorship, especially when both mentor and mentee have demanding schedules. Establishing realistic time commitments and being transparent about availability are essential. Setting boundaries, scheduling regular check-ins, and respecting each other's time constraints contribute to a balanced and sustainable mentorship dynamic.

3. Adapting to Changing Circumstances:

The cybersecurity landscape is dynamic, and circumstances may change for both mentor and mentee. Career shifts, personal obligations, or unforeseen challenges may impact the mentorship relationship. Being adaptable and understanding of changing circumstances is crucial. Open communication allows both parties to navigate these changes collaboratively and maintain the resilience of the mentorship.

4. Seeking Additional Mentoring Resources:

In some cases, a single mentor may not cover all aspects of a mentee's multifaceted career journey. Encouraging mentees to seek additional resources, such as industry-specific forums, peer networks, or specialized mentors for specific skill areas, enhances the diversity and depth of their support network.

Conclusion: Nurturing Mentorship for Cybersecurity Success

In conclusion, finding a mentor and engaging in structured mentorship programs are pivotal steps in launching a successful cybersecurity career. The guidance, knowledge transfer, and networking opportunities that stem from mentorship can significantly accelerate professional development. By approaching mentorship strategically, participating in mentoring programs, and fostering mutually beneficial relationships, individuals can navigate the complexities of the cybersecurity landscape with confidence.

As you embark on your journey of finding a mentor and embracing mentorship, may each interaction be a catalyst for growth, resilience, and success in the ever-evolving world of cybersecurity. Remember that mentorship is a continuous journey of learning, collaboration, and shared accomplishments that contribute to the collective strength and advancement of the cybersecurity community.

Chapter 9: Advancing Your Career

Specialization and Advanced Training

Cloud Security and Incident Response and Forensics

In the ever-evolving landscape of cybersecurity, advancing your career requires a strategic focus on specialization and advanced training. This chapter explores two critical subtopics: Cloud Security and Incident Response and Forensics. As an experienced cybersecurity professional, I recognize the pivotal role these specializations play in shaping a successful and impactful career.

Cloud Security: Navigating the Digital Skies

1. The Significance of Cloud Security:

As organizations increasingly embrace cloud computing, the importance of securing cloud environments becomes paramount. Cloud security involves protecting data, applications, and infrastructure in cloud environments from evolving cyber threats. With major cloud service providers like AWS, Azure, and Google Cloud dominating the digital landscape, professionals specializing in cloud security are in high demand.

2. Key Concepts in Cloud Security:

Understanding the foundational concepts of cloud security is crucial for professionals aiming to specialize in this field. This includes knowledge of shared responsibility models, identity and access management (IAM), encryption mechanisms, secure configuration practices, and compliance frameworks relevant to cloud environments.

3. Cloud Service Models and Deployment Models:

Cloud security professionals must comprehend various cloud service models (IaaS, PaaS, SaaS) and deployment models (public, private, hybrid). Each model introduces unique security considerations, and proficiency in adapting security controls to these models is essential. A deep understanding allows professionals to design robust and tailored security solutions.

4. Skills and Certifications in Cloud Security:

Developing technical skills in cloud security tools and platforms is fundamental. Familiarity with tools like AWS Security Hub, Azure Security Center, and Google Cloud Security Command Center is valuable. Certifications such as the AWS Certified Security – Specialty, Certified Cloud Security Professional (CCSP), and Google Cloud Professional Security Engineer enhance credibility and demonstrate expertise in cloud security.

5. Continuous Learning in a Dynamic Landscape:

Cloud technology evolves rapidly, necessitating a commitment to continuous learning. Professionals should stay updated on the latest cloud security trends, emerging threats, and advancements in cloud platforms. Engaging in cloud-focused communities, attending webinars, and pursuing advanced certifications contribute to ongoing professional development.

Incident Response and Forensics: Unravelling the Digital Puzzle

1. The Crucial Role of Incident Response and Forensics:

In the face of cyber threats, organizations rely on incident response and digital forensics to identify, contain, and recover from security incidents. These specializations play a crucial role in unravelling the complexities of cyberattacks, understanding their origins, and implementing measures to prevent future incidents.

2. Incident Response Lifecycle:

Proficiency in the incident response lifecycle is foundational. This includes preparation, identification, containment, eradication, recovery, and lessons learned. Professionals specializing in incident response must be adept at crafting and executing incident response plans tailored to their organization's unique risk profile.

3. Digital Forensics Techniques:

Digital forensics involves the systematic collection, analysis, and preservation of digital evidence. Specialized skills in using forensic tools, analyzing network logs, and conducting memory forensics are crucial. Understanding file systems, metadata, and the intricacies of digital artifacts is essential for uncovering the full scope of a security incident.

4. Collaboration and Communication:

Effective incident response requires collaboration across departments and seamless communication. Professionals in this field must excel in coordinating efforts among IT, legal, and executive teams. Clear and concise communication during incident investigations ensures a swift and coordinated response to minimize the impact of security incidents.

5. Certifications in Incident Response and Forensics:

Industry-recognized certifications validate expertise in incident response and forensics. Certifications like the Certified Incident Handler (ECIH), Certified Digital Forensics Examiner (CDFE), and GIAC Certified Incident Handler (GCIH) enhance professional credibility and demonstrate a commitment to excellence in these specializations.

Developing Expertise in Both Specializations: A Holistic Approach

1. Overlapping Skills:

Cloud security and incident response/forensics, though distinct, share overlapping skills. Proficiency in networking, knowledge of operating systems, and a deep understanding of cybersecurity principles are foundational for success in both specializations. Professionals can leverage these common skills to develop expertise in both areas.

2. Integration of Specializations:

Cybersecurity professionals often encounter scenarios where cloud security and incident response intersect. An organization's cloud environment may be a target for cyberattacks, requiring professionals to seamlessly integrate cloud security measures with incident response strategies. Understanding how these specializations complement each other is invaluable.

3. Hybrid Roles and Career Paths:

Some professionals opt for hybrid roles that blend expertise in cloud security and incident response/forensics. Such roles may involve overseeing the security of cloud environments while also leading incident response teams. Navigating a hybrid career path requires a diverse skill set and the ability to adapt to the evolving demands of both specializations.

4. Strategic Training and Certifications:

Training programs and certifications that encompass both cloud security and incident response/forensics contribute to a well-rounded skill set. Professionals can strategically select certifications that bridge these specializations, such as the Certified Cloud Forensics Professional (CCFP) or the Certified Cloud Security Professional (CCSP).

Challenges and Growth Opportunities

1. Addressing the Challenges of Rapid Technological Advancements:

Both cloud security and incident response/forensics operate in an environment of rapid technological advancements. Professionals must stay ahead of evolving threats and technologies, necessitating a commitment to continuous learning. The challenge lies in balancing the need for expertise with the dynamic nature of the cybersecurity landscape.

2. Cultivating a Proactive Mindset:

Success in both specializations requires a proactive mindset. Professionals should anticipate emerging threats in cloud environments and continuously refine incident response plans to address evolving attack vectors. Embracing a proactive approach positions individuals as leaders in shaping robust cybersecurity postures for organizations.

3. Global Collaboration and Information Sharing:

Cybersecurity is a global challenge, and professionals in both specializations benefit from global collaboration and information sharing. Engaging with international cybersecurity communities, participating in threat intelligence forums, and contributing to industry discussions amplify collective knowledge and foster growth opportunities.

4. Diversity of Perspectives and Solutions:

Embracing diversity of perspectives is essential for tackling the complex challenges in cloud security and incident response/forensics. Professionals should actively seek out diverse viewpoints, engage in collaborative problem-solving, and contribute to the development of innovative solutions that address the multifaceted nature of cybersecurity threats.

Conclusion: Paving the Way for an Advanced Cybersecurity Career

In conclusion, specialization in cloud security and incident response/forensics is a strategic pathway to advancing a cybersecurity career. The dynamic nature of these specializations requires professionals to stay agile, continuously learn, and adapt to the evolving threat landscape. By developing expertise in both cloud security and incident response, professionals can navigate complex challenges, contribute to global cybersecurity efforts, and play a pivotal role in securing digital environments.

As you embark on the journey of specialization and advanced training, may each skill acquired, and certification earned be a stepping stone toward an advanced and impactful cybersecurity career. The intersection of cloud security and incident response/forensics represents a frontier of opportunities for professionals committed to shaping the future of cybersecurity.

Blogging and Thought Leadership, Contributing to the Community

In the dynamic and competitive field of cybersecurity, building a strong professional brand is a strategic imperative for career advancement. This chapter explores two vital subtopics: Blogging and Thought Leadership and Contributing to the Community. As an experienced cybersecurity professional, I recognize the transformative power of a well-crafted professional brand in shaping a successful and fulfilling career.

Building a Professional Brand: A Strategic Imperative

1. The Significance of a Professional Brand:

In the cybersecurity landscape, where talent is highly sought after, establishing a strong professional brand sets individuals apart in a crowded field. A professional brand is the amalgamation of one's expertise, reputation, and unique contributions to the cybersecurity community. It serves as a testament to your skills, knowledge, and the value you bring to the industry.

2. Trust and Credibility:

A well-defined professional brand fosters trust and credibility among peers, employers, and the broader cybersecurity community. As organizations seek professionals with proven expertise, a strong brand signals reliability and competence. Trust is a cornerstone in the cybersecurity domain, and a robust professional brand contributes significantly to building that trust.

3. Visibility and Recognition:

Building a professional brand enhances visibility and recognition within the industry. Whether you are seeking career opportunities, collaborations, or speaking engagements, a recognizable brand opens doors. It positions you as an authority in your niche, leading to increased opportunities for networking, mentorship, and participation in high-impact cybersecurity initiatives.

4. Career Advancement:

A strategically built professional brand is a catalyst for career advancement. Employers are more likely to consider individuals with a visible and impactful presence in the cybersecurity community. Whether climbing the corporate ladder or exploring entrepreneurial endeavors, a strong brand acts as a powerful asset, attracting opportunities aligned with your career goals.

Blogging and Thought Leadership: Crafting Your Digital Voice

1. The Power of Blogging in Cybersecurity:

Blogging is a dynamic platform for cybersecurity professionals to share insights, expertise, and thought leadership. Through blogging, you can contribute valuable content to the community, establish yourself as a subject matter expert, and create a digital footprint that resonates with your target audience.

2. Identifying Your Niche:

Before diving into blogging, identify your niche within the vast cybersecurity landscape. Whether it's ethical hacking, threat intelligence, cloud security, or any specialized area, narrowing your focus allows you to provide in-depth and targeted content. A defined niche helps you stand out and attracts an audience interested in your specific expertise.

3. Crafting Engaging and Educational Content:

Effective blogging goes beyond sharing experiences; it involves crafting content that engages and educates your audience. Whether you're breaking down complex cybersecurity concepts, sharing hands-on experiences, or offering insights into emerging threats, your content should provide value and resonate with both beginners and seasoned professionals.

4. Consistency and Building Authority:

Consistency is key in blogging. Regularly publishing high-quality content not only keeps your audience engaged but also contributes to building your authority in the field. As your blog gains traction, your insights become a go-to resource for professionals seeking knowledge, further establishing your position as a thought leader.

5. Engaging with Your Audience:

A successful blog is not a one-way street. Actively engage with your audience through comments, social media, and other platforms. Respond to questions, participate in discussions, and seek feedback. This two-way interaction not only strengthens your connection with the community but also provides valuable insights into the interests and concerns of your audience.

6. Utilizing Multiple Platforms:

Beyond traditional blogging, leverage other platforms to amplify your reach. Consider contributing guest posts to reputable cybersecurity websites, participating in podcast interviews, or creating video content. Diversifying your content across multiple platforms enhances your visibility and caters to different preferences within the cybersecurity community.

7. Showcasing Practical Experience:

Share practical experiences and real-world scenarios in your blog. Practical insights, case studies, and hands-on examples resonate well with cybersecurity professionals who are looking for actionable information. Demonstrating your ability to apply theoretical knowledge to real-world situations adds credibility to your brand.

Contributing to the Community: A Collective Growth Approach

1. Community Involvement and Collaboration:

Contributing to the cybersecurity community involves active involvement and collaboration. Engage in forums, discussion groups, and social media platforms where cybersecurity professionals congregate. Share your knowledge, participate in conversations, and contribute to the collective growth of the community.

2. Mentorship and Knowledge Sharing:

Actively participating in mentorship and knowledge-sharing initiatives strengthens your ties with the community. Whether through formal mentoring programs, online forums, or personal engagements, offering guidance to aspiring professionals fosters a culture of continuous learning and growth. Your contributions as a mentor contribute to the development of the next generation of cybersecurity leaders.

3. Open-Source Contributions:

Open-source projects are at the heart of cybersecurity innovation. Contribute to open-source initiatives, share your expertise, and collaborate with like-minded professionals on projects that align with your interests. Open-source contributions not only enhance your visibility but also contribute to the collective improvement of cybersecurity tools and practices.

4. Speaking Engagements and Webinars:

Share your insights and expertise through speaking engagements at conferences, webinars, and industry events. Presenting at reputable forums not only establishes you as a thought leader but also provides a platform to connect with industry professionals. Engaging with diverse audiences contributes to the expansion of your network and reinforces your professional brand.

5. Writing for Publications:

Contribute articles and research papers to reputable cybersecurity publications. Writing for established publications enhances your credibility and positions you as a trusted source of information. It also provides an avenue to reach a broader audience and contribute to the ongoing discourse within the cybersecurity community.

6. Collaborative Initiatives and Projects:

Collaborate with fellow professionals on initiatives and projects that address cybersecurity challenges. Whether it's conducting research, developing tools, or organizing community events, collaborative efforts demonstrate your commitment to the collective betterment of the cybersecurity landscape. Such initiatives contribute to your professional brand as a team player and innovator.

Challenges and Growth Opportunities

1. Navigating Time Constraints:

Building a professional brand through blogging and community contributions requires time and commitment. Balancing these activities with professional responsibilities can be challenging. Prioritize effectively, establish a schedule, and allocate dedicated time to building your brand to overcome this challenge.

2. Overcoming Imposter Syndrome:

Imposter syndrome, a common challenge in the cybersecurity field, may hinder professionals from actively engaging in thought leadership and community contributions. Recognize your accomplishments, embrace your unique perspective, and understand that everyone has something valuable to contribute. Overcoming imposter syndrome is an essential step toward building a strong professional brand.

3. Staying Relevant in a Dynamic Landscape:

The cybersecurity landscape evolves rapidly, and staying relevant is an ongoing challenge. Embrace continuous learning, monitor industry trends, and adapt your content and contributions to reflect the latest developments. Staying informed ensures that your professional brand remains current and aligned with the ever-changing cybersecurity environment.

4. Handling Criticism and Feedback:

Publicly sharing your insights invites both positive feedback and constructive criticism. Handle feedback gracefully, view it as an opportunity for growth, and use it to refine your perspectives and content. Responding professionally to criticism contributes to the resilience of your professional brand.

Conclusion: Crafting Your Cybersecurity Narrative

In conclusion, building a professional brand through blogging, thought leadership, and community contributions is a strategic pathway to advancing your cybersecurity career. By establishing a strong digital presence, sharing valuable insights, and actively contributing to the community, you shape a narrative that resonates with your professional goals and aspirations.

As you embark on the journey of building your professional brand, may each blog post, community contribution, and collaborative initiative be a building block toward a distinguished cybersecurity career. Remember that your unique perspective and contributions play a crucial role in the collective growth of the cybersecurity community. In a field where collaboration and knowledge-sharing are paramount, your voice adds valuable depth to the ongoing cybersecurity discourse.

Chapter 10: Facing Challenges and Staying Resilient

Ethical Dilemmas in Cybersecurity, Handling Burnout and Stress, Continuous Adaptation to the Evolving Landscape

In the dynamic and complex realm of cybersecurity, professionals often face a multitude of challenges that require resilience and adaptability. This chapter explores three critical topics: Ethical Dilemmas in Cybersecurity, Handling Burnout and Stress, and Continuous Adaptation to the Evolving Landscape. Drawing upon my experience as a seasoned cybersecurity professional, I aim to provide insights and strategies to navigate these challenges effectively.

Ethical Dilemmas in Cybersecurity: Navigating the Gray Areas

1. The Ethical Landscape of Cybersecurity:

Cybersecurity professionals are entrusted with safeguarding digital assets, often requiring ethical decision-making in the face of evolving threats. Ethical dilemmas can arise in areas such as vulnerability disclosure, incident response, and offensive security practices. It is crucial for professionals to navigate these gray areas with a commitment to integrity and ethical conduct.

2. Vulnerability Disclosure and Responsible Disclosure Policies:

One common ethical dilemma involves the responsible disclosure of vulnerabilities. Cybersecurity researchers often discover vulnerabilities in systems, and deciding when and how to disclose such findings requires careful consideration. Adhering to responsible disclosure policies, collaborating with affected parties, and prioritizing the security of end-users are essential elements of ethical decision-making in this context.

3. Balancing Offensive Security Practices:

Professionals engaged in offensive security practices, such as penetration testing and ethical hacking, encounter ethical considerations. Striking a balance between uncovering vulnerabilities for improvement and ensuring that actions do not harm systems or violate privacy is challenging. Adhering to ethical guidelines, obtaining proper authorization, and maintaining transparency are crucial in mitigating ethical concerns.

4. The Human Element in Incident Response:

Incident response scenarios often involve human actors, adding complexity to ethical considerations. Balancing the need to investigate and mitigate security incidents with respect for individuals' privacy and rights is paramount. Professionals must approach incident response ethically, ensuring that actions align with legal frameworks and ethical standards.

5. Continuous Ethical Awareness:

Ethical decision-making is an ongoing process that requires continuous awareness and reflection. Cybersecurity professionals should stay informed about evolving ethical standards, industry best practices, and legal regulations. Engaging in ethical discussions within the cybersecurity community and seeking mentorship can provide valuable perspectives for navigating complex ethical dilemmas.

Handling Burnout and Stress: Sustaining Well-Being in a High-Stakes Environment

1. The High-Stakes Environment of Cybersecurity:

The nature of cybersecurity work, with its constant vigilance against threats and the potential for high-impact incidents, can lead to stress and burnout. Professionals in this field must proactively address these challenges to sustain their well-being and maintain peak performance.

2. Recognizing Burnout Warning Signs:

Burnout is a gradual process, and recognizing warning signs early is crucial. Persistent fatigue, decreased motivation, irritability, and changes in sleep patterns are indicators of burnout. Cybersecurity professionals should be attuned to these signs, both in themselves and their colleagues, to intervene effectively.

3. Balancing Workload and Prioritizing Tasks:

Balancing the workload in a field where the volume and complexity of tasks can be overwhelming is essential. Prioritizing tasks based on urgency and importance, setting realistic goals, and establishing healthy work boundaries contribute to a sustainable workload. Learning to say no when necessary is a skill that can prevent burnout.

4. Embracing Stress Management Techniques:

Stress management is integral to maintaining well-being. Cybersecurity professionals can adopt various techniques such as mindfulness, meditation, exercise, and hobbies to manage stress. Establishing a healthy work-life balance, taking breaks, and incorporating stress-relief practices into daily routines contribute to long-term resilience.

5. Building Support Networks:

Building and nurturing support networks is crucial in times of stress. Cybersecurity professionals should foster open communication with colleagues, managers, and mentors. Peer support, mentorship, and sharing experiences can create a sense of community and provide valuable insights into coping strategies.

6. Seeking Professional Assistance:

In cases of persistent burnout or overwhelming stress, seeking professional assistance is a proactive step. Mental health professionals, counsellors, or employee assistance programs can provide guidance and support. Destigmatizing mental health discussions within the cybersecurity community contributes to a healthier and more resilient workforce.

Continuous Adaptation to the Evolving Landscape: Embracing a Learning Mindset

1. The Dynamic Nature of Cybersecurity:

The cybersecurity landscape is in a perpetual state of evolution, with new threats, technologies, and vulnerabilities emerging regularly. Cybersecurity professionals must embrace a learning mindset to stay relevant and effective in their roles.

2. Continuous Learning and Professional Development:

Continuous learning is a cornerstone of success in cybersecurity. Professionals should actively pursue opportunities for professional development, whether through formal education, certifications, workshops, or hands-on training. Staying abreast of industry trends and advancements is essential for adapting to the evolving threat landscape.

3. Participating in Knowledge-Sharing Communities:

Engaging in knowledge-sharing communities within the cybersecurity field enhances continuous learning. Forums, conferences, webinars, and online communities provide platforms for professionals to exchange insights, discuss emerging trends, and collaborate on solutions. Actively participating in these forums contributes to a collective understanding of the evolving landscape.

4. Experimentation and Practical Application:

The hands-on nature of cybersecurity requires professionals to experiment with new tools, techniques, and methodologies. Creating a conducive environment for experimentation, such as a home lab, allows professionals to gain practical experience and test their skills in a controlled setting. Practical application reinforces theoretical knowledge and fosters adaptability.

5. Adapting Security Postures:

Organizations must continually adapt their security postures to respond to evolving threats. Cybersecurity professionals play a vital role in assessing and adjusting security measures based on the current threat landscape. Proactive risk assessments, threat intelligence analysis, and collaboration with stakeholders contribute to a dynamic and adaptive security posture.

6. Agile and Collaborative Approaches:

Embracing agile methodologies and collaborative approaches enhances adaptability. Cybersecurity professionals should work closely with cross-functional teams, incorporating security measures into development processes, and adapting strategies based on feedback and emerging threat intelligence. Collaboration fosters a culture of continuous improvement and adaptation.

Challenges and Growth Opportunities

1. Navigating Ethical Gray Areas:

Ethical dilemmas in cybersecurity pose challenges that require careful navigation. Professionals must continually educate themselves on ethical standards, seek diverse perspectives, and engage in open discussions to make informed and ethical decisions. Navigating these challenges provides opportunities for personal and professional growth.

2. Fostering Resilience Against Burnout:

Building resilience against burnout is an ongoing process that involves self-awareness and proactive measures. Cybersecurity professionals should view challenges as opportunities for growth, implement effective stress management techniques, and foster a supportive network. Overcoming burnout contributes to long-term career sustainability.

3. Adapting to Rapid Technological Changes:

The rapid pace of technological change presents both challenges and growth opportunities. Professionals who embrace continuous learning, experiment with new technologies, and stay engaged with knowledge-sharing communities position themselves as adaptable and resourceful contributors to the cybersecurity landscape.

4. Strategic Approaches to Well-Being:

The challenges of well-being in cybersecurity require strategic approaches. Professionals should integrate stress management practices into their daily routines, seek professional assistance when needed, and foster a culture within organizations that prioritizes mental health. Prioritizing well-being contributes to sustained success in the field.

Conclusion: Navigating Challenges with Resilience

In conclusion, facing challenges and staying resilient is an inherent part of a cybersecurity professional's journey. Ethical dilemmas, burnout, and the dynamic nature of the field present hurdles that, when navigated with resilience and adaptability, contribute to personal and professional growth. As you confront these challenges, remember that each experience is an opportunity to refine your skills, strengthen your character, and shape a fulfilling and impactful career in cybersecurity.

References

https://www.coursera.org/articles/cybersecurity-career-paths

https://www.cyberseek.org/pathway.html

https://www.cybersecurityeducation.org/careers/

https://www.geeksforgeeks.org/tcp-ip-model/

https://www.geeksforgeeks.org/linux-tutorial/

https://www.geeksforgeeks.org/windows-tutorial/

A Request to The Reader

Hey Reader,

Exciting times! As you check out "Cybersecurity Blueprint," I've got a favour to ask. This book is like a roadmap for getting into cybersecurity, and I want to know what you think. Any 'lightbulb moments' or challenges you faced—share them with me. Your positive vibes and thoughts aren't just a boost for me; they help future readers too. Your feedback guides where this book goes next. So, while you're reading, know that your thoughts make a real difference. Thanks a bunch for joining in on this cybersecurity journey!

Cheers,

Afrin Shaik,

Cyber Security Professional.